THE LIFE OF BLESSED BERNARD OF TIRON

GEOFFREY GROSSUS

THE LIFE OF BLESSED BERNARD OF TIRON

Translated with an introduction and notes by

RUTH HARWOOD CLINE

The Catholic University of America Press
Washington, D.C.

The paper used in this publication meets the minimum
requirements of American National Standards for Information
Science—Permanence of Paper for Printed Library Materials,
ANSI Z39.48-1984.
∞

Library of Congress Cataloging-in-Publication Data
Grossus, Geoffrey, 12th cent.
[Vita B. Bernardi Tironiensis. English]
The life of Blessed Bernard of Tiron / Geoffrey Grossus ;
translated with an introduction and notes by
Ruth Harwood Cline.
p. cm.
Includes bibliographical references and index.
ISBN 978-0-8132-1681-2 (pbk. : alk. paper) 1. Bernard, de
Tiron, Saint, ca. 1046–1116 or 17. I. Title.
BX4700.B457G7613 2009
282.092—dc22
[B]
2009008079

To my youngest grandchildren:
Joseph William Francis, Annemarie Rose Thérèse,
and Geoffrey Nathanael John le Grelle

Contents

Acknowledgments

I am deeply indebted to Jo Ann Moran Cruz and Bennett Hill, my doctoral advisers on the twelfth-century foundation and expansion of the congregation of Tiron, and to my third adviser, Theodore Evergates, for his expert editing of the introduction. Joseph Tylenda, S.J., director of Woodstock Library, Georgetown University; Bruce Miller, coordinator of the Religious Studies library, Mullen Library, the Catholic University of America; John Hardacre, the Winchester Cathedral librarian; and the librarians of Georgetown University, the Catholic University of America, the Library of Congress, the Bibliothèque Nationale, the British Library, the Médiathèque François Mitterrand, the Centre d'Etudes Supérieures de Civilisation Médievale of Poitiers, and the Universities of Edinburgh and Glasgow, were most helpful; Suzanne Foster of the Winchester College Library made twelfth-century charters available. In Chartres, Abbé Pierre Bizeau, the diocesan archivist, and Michel Thibault, the departmental archivist, and in Poitiers, Mirielle Jean, the departmental archivist, offered valuable guidance. Geoffrey Barrow, Mark Dilworth, and Kenneth Varty guided my researches on Tironian abbeys in Scotland. Dennis McManus of Georgetown University advised on the Latin text. Giles Constable, professor emeritus at the School of Historical Studies, Institute for Advanced Study, Princeton, New Jersey, showed sustained interest. Constance Berman, professor of history, University of Iowa, advised on Tiron's development into an order. Constance Brittain Bouchard, distinguished professor of medieval history, University of Akron, Ohio, advised on the Grossi family. I am most grateful for their time and expertise.

RUTH HARWOOD CLINE
Georgetown University, Washington, D.C.

Introduction

Bernard of Tiron (ca. 1046–1116) and Robert of Arbrissel (ca. 1045–1116), founder of Fontevraud (1101), were among the most influential monastic reformers of their time, but Bernard has drawn less scholarly attention. Bernard of Tiron, founder of Tiron Abbey (1107) (diocese of Chartres, 12.8 kilometers, or 7.7 miles, east of Nogent-le-Rotrou in Perche) and of distant priories in Beaujolais and the British Isles, remains largely unknown even to historians of Western monasticism. Bernard's life as a monk was both typical and exceptional. He was a scholar of Scripture and trained in canon law, but also skilled in woodworking and ironwork and engaged in trade. A charismatic leader, a renegade, a sympathetic confessor, a healer, and a visionary, he was strongly supported by Henry I, king of England, and his extensive noble kinship group, and was once venerated throughout modern France.[1] He strictly observed the *Rule of Saint Benedict*[2] as a prior and abbot, but during unauthorized absences from the cloister he was also a hermit and traveling preacher who was embroiled in numerous conflicts

1. Andreas of Fontevraud, *Vita Altera* of Robert of Arbrissel, 15, *Acta Sanctorum* (hereafter AASS), Feb. 3: 0611A, describes "Abbot Bernard, of worthy memory of all good persons, praised continuously today [before 1120] by all the religious establishments of Gaul." *"Abbas Bernardus bonorum omnium memoria dignus, cuius laus usque hodie per omnes Galliae Ecclesias."* (Hereafter AASS citations, and the Latin text of the *vita,* are from the Acta Sanctorum Database 1999–2006 ProQuest Information and Learning Company.)

2. Benedict of Monte Cassino, *The Rule of Saint Benedict,* ed. Timothy Fry (Collegeville, Minn.: Liturgical Press, 1981) (hereafter *RB*).

related to the religious reform movements of the late eleventh century. After his death, Tiron Abbey became the mother house of a monastic order consisting of eight abbeys in France, four in Scotland, one in Wales, and more than one hundred priories. The congregation of Tiron survived almost seven centuries, until the French Revolution, and has since passed into obscurity.[3]

The *Vita*

The *Vita B. Bernardi Tironiensis* was commissioned by, and in turn dedicated to, Geoffrey II of Lèves, bishop of Chartres, who had known Bernard at least since 1114 and may have intended to promote his canonization in Rome. The author of the *vita,* Geoffrey Grossus,[4] far from being "least of all monks," as he modestly wrote, perhaps served as Tiron's chancellor.[5] The *vita,* written around 1147, is known today through sixteenth- and seventeenth-century copies of a late thirteenth-century version.[6] Jean-Baptiste Souchet, a canon of the cathedral of Chartres, first printed an annotated edition in 1649.[7] In 1675, the Bollandist

3. Ruth Harwood Cline, "The Congregation of Tiron in the Twelfth Century: Foundation and Expansion" (Ph.D. diss., Georgetown University, 2000), 520. The evidence is available in this doctoral dissertation and will be presented in greater detail in a forthcoming monograph.

4. See Constance Brittain Bouchard, *Sword, Miter, and Cloister: Nobility and the Church in Burgundy, 980–1198* (Ithaca, N.Y.: Cornell University Press, 1981), 300–303. The Grossi were the lords of Uxelles and also lords of Brancion, a family that had two brothers who were successively claustral priors at Cluny. Since Bouchard found no connection between Geoffrey and Walter Grossus, monks of Tiron, and this Burgundian family, whether Grossus is a family name or a nickname meaning "big" or "fat" is uncertain.

5. Lucien Merlet, ed., *Cartulaire de l'Abbaye de la Sainte-Trinité de Tiron* (Chartres: Imprimerie Garnier, 1883), 1:99, no. 79.

6. Geoffrey's autograph manuscript was copied by Jean Pignore de Vallea at the order of John of Chartres, abbot of Tiron (1290–1297). Additional handwritten copies were made of this thirteenth-century copy in the sixteenth and seventeenth centuries, when they were combined with other literature about Bernard of Tiron: the Synopsis, Sermon, and Prayer. See Bernard Beck, *Saint-Bernard de Tiron, l'ermite, le moine et le monde* (Cormelles-le-Royal: La Mandragore, 1998), 35–39. Two surviving manuscripts are Paris: BNF Fonds Latin 13788, ca. 1630, and Rome: Bibliotheca Apostolica Vaticana, Reg. 526, fols. 1–86, dated 1656.

7. Geoffroy le Gros, *B. Bernardi, fundatoris et primi abbatis SS Trinitatis de*

Geoffrey Henskens reprinted it in a new format with notes in *Acta Sanctorum,* and in 1854 Jacques-Paul Migne published the *vita* in *Patrologia Latina.*[8]

In a flowery prologue, Geoffrey described his sources. He explained that he was writing up his eyewitness notes on the founder of Tiron and incorporating other material from reliable correspondents. Although the *vita* is written in the first person, the inconsistencies, including in names, suggest a tendency on Geoffrey's part to incorporate materials without substantive change. The sources incorporated may have included a member of the hermit community headed by Vital of Savigny and a provider of inaccurate material concerning Bernard's years at Saint-Cyprien of Poitiers and its daughter abbey of Saint-Savin-sur-Gartempe.[9] The *vita* contains extensive borrowings from St. Jerome's epitaph letter praising St. Paula (d. 404) and mourning her death,[10] with Bernard's name substituted for that of the Roman widow and mother. Difficulties in dating some of this fragmented information are in part due to the fact that Geoffrey organized the entire *vita* in a classical pedimental composition, a harmonious literary arrangement.[11] The double episodes are most apparent at the cen-

---

Tironio Vita, ed. Jean-Baptiste Souchet (Paris: Billaine, 1649, 1680), 35, n. 1, and 473.

8. Geoffrey Grossus, *Vita beati Bernardi Tironiensis auctore Gaufredo Grosso,* eds. Godefroy Henskens and Daniel Papebroch, AASS, Apr. 2 (Antwerp: Joannem Mevrsium, 1643, 1675), 0222C–0255A. Grossus, *Vita beati Bernardi Fundatoris Congregationis de Tironio in Gallia auctore Gaufredo Grosso,* ed. Jacques-Paul Migne, in *Patrologia Latina* 172 (Paris: Garnier, 1854), 1362–1446D. (Hereafter PL; citations are from the Patrologia Latina Database 1996–2007 ProQuest Information and Learning Company.)

9. For inaccuracies in the early years, see the notes to the text.

10. Jerome, "Ad Eustochium Virginem Epitaphium Paulae Matris," in *Sancti Eusebii Hieronymi Epistulae, Pars II, Epistulae LXXI–CXX,* ed. Isidorus Hilberg, *Corpus Scriptorum Ecclesiasticorum Latinorum* (hereafter CSEL), vol. 55 (Vienna: 1996), 306–51, no. 108.

11. Chiasmus is an ancient rhetorical device defined in the Random House Unabridged Dictionary as "a reversal in the order of words in two otherwise parallel phrases"; (§11): "an opponent of injustice and of justice a proponent." Similar parallelism of events leading up to and away from the central event is present in pedimental composition. See Mary Douglas, *Thinking in Circles, An Essay on Ring Composition* (New Haven, Conn.: Yale University Press, 2007), xii–xiv, who credits John L. Myres for the term, in *Herodotus, Father of History* (Oxford: Clarendon Press, 1953).

ter of the structure, where a single journey to Rome is described as two trips. While esthetically pleasing, this structure causes difficulties in dating some of this fragmented information.

Bernard's birth
 Schooling
  Monastic life
   Hermit life (Saint-Médard)
    Chausey Island, pirates
     Return to monastic life
      Abbot (Saint-Cyprien)
       Preaching (Normandy)
        Trip to Rome
         Private audience with Pope Paschal II
        Trip to Rome
       Address to curia
      Abbot (Saint-Cyprien)
     Departure from monastic life
    Chausey Island, pirates
   Hermit life (Chennedet)
  Tiron Abbey founded
 School at Tiron
Bernard's death

Whether or not Bishop Geoffrey II requested Bernard's *vita* as part of a canonization process, Geoffrey Grossus presented Bernard as destined for sainthood. According to Geoffrey, Bernard was a soldier and imitator of Christ. He was a bloodless martyr by virtue of his chastity, abstinence, and generosity. As an abbot, he was a worthy successor of St. Benedict of Monte Cassino and St. Benedict of Aniane by both the example of his life and his strict observance of the *Rule*. His spirituality, healings, efficacious prayers, prophetic spirit, and visions were remarkable and more than compensated for the relatively few miracles attributed to him.[12]

12. Cline, "Congregation of Tiron," 221–77.

Although this remarkable *vita* is frequently used as a primary source, its historical accuracy should not be accepted unquestioningly. The *vita* is inaccurate in important ways, particularly with regard to material for Poitiers. While the *vita* states that Bernard professed as a monk at Saint-Cyprien, as shown in the chronology c. 1073, his earliest spiritual mentors, Hildebert and Garnier, from Montmorillon near Poitiers, were monks of Chaise-Dieu.[13] Thus Bernard may have professed as a monk at Chaise-Dieu and accompanied Renaud to Saint-Cyprien of Poitiers in 1073. Although an unnamed abbot of Saint-Savin was convicted of simony in 1080 and fled,[14] as indicated in the chronology, the *vita*'s assertion that he was Gervais is doubtful, for Gervais was prior of Saint-Cyprien as late as 1081. Gervais witnessed local charters as abbot of Saint-Savin from 1082 until his departure for the Holy Land after 1095, disproving the *vita*'s description of his abandonment of the abbey to Bernard, the claustral prior.[15] The description of the Council of Poitiers is borrowed from the Chronicle of Hugh of Flavigny (c. 1103) and William of Malmesbury's (d. 1143) *Gesta Regum Anglorum* (1120), and Bernard is given the role actually played by the papal legates. The *vita*'s claim that the pope restored Bernard as abbot of Saint-Cyprien is disproved by an abbey charter.[16] Saint-Cyprien recovered its independence at a later date, but the abbot was not Bernard.[17] In contrast, the *vita*'s de-

13. Robert Favreau et al., *Saint-Savin, l'Abbaye et ses Peintures Murales* (Poitiers: Connaissance et promotion du patrimoine de Poitou-Charentes, 1999), 17, n. 60. The only source placing them at Saint-Cyprian is the *vita* itself.

14. *Recueil des Historiens des Gaules et de la France,* ed. Michel-Jean-Joseph Brial, new edition (Paris: Palmé, 1877), 14:670–71. Letter from Amatus of Oloron, papal legate, directing Ralph, archbishop of Tours, who had just convened the Council of Bordeaux in October 1080, to take the abbot captive and return him with the stolen property to the bishop of Poitiers.

15. Favreau, *Saint-Savin,* 16–17.

16. The abbey's cartulary states that Bernard pled his case in Rome without results, returned, and soon departed for the wilderness (Louis Rédet, ed., *Cartulaire de l'Abbaye de Saint-Cyprien de Poitiers,* Archives Historiques du Poitou [Poitiers: Oudin, 1874], 3: 46, no. 43).

17. As early as 1004, Abbo, abbot of Fleury, wrote to Odilon, abbot of Cluny, regarding Cluny's oversight of Saint-Cyprien (PL, 139, 0438C–049B). Stephen IX

scription of the foundation and expansion of Tiron with support from many benefactors is corroborated by the cartulary of Tiron and the correspondence of Ivo, bishop of Chartres.

In addition to inaccuracies, the *vita* also has important inconsistencies and omissions. Geoffrey both vilified William, duke of Aquitaine, as "the enemy of all decency and holiness" (§48) and praised him as a benefactor (§98). Although Geoffrey devoted one chapter to Bernard's prayerful battle with the Devil for the souls of the merchants and pirates and two chapters to Bernard's pious death, he played down important events, such as Bernard's meeting with Henry I, in order to focus on Bernard's holiness. Geoffrey also omitted information about Bernard contained in two contemporary saints' lives: his travels with Robert of Arbrissel shortly before their deaths and the miraculous release of the crusader St. Adjutor through Bernard's posthumous intercession.[18] The *vita*'s combination of realistic description and echoes of earlier saints' lives makes it a skillfully presented hagiography of an abbot who deserved canonization because of his spiritual gifts and holy life. Nonetheless, absolute truthfulness and completeness were not necessarily standards for hagiography, an inspirational rather than historical genre, and the *vita* must be cited selectively as a primary source.

Monastic Reform

The foundation of Tiron Abbey by Bernard of Abbeville was part of wider movements of monastic reform in Europe in the

---

and Gregory VII referred vaguely to such a right in 1058 and 1075 (*Bullarium Cluniacense,* 16.1, 19.1). Pascal II listed Saint-Cyprien as an abbey subject to Cluny on November 20, 1100 (*Bullarium Cluniacense* 32.2). Dietrich W. Poeck, *Cluniacensis Ecclesia, Der cluniacensische Klosterverband (10.–12. Jahrhundert),* Münstersche Mittelalter-Schriften, vol. 71 (Munich: Wilhelm Fink Verlag, 1998), 91, notes that the papal privilege issued by Honorius II (1124–1130) on April 2, 1125, (*Bullarium Cluniacense* 42), is the last Cluniac claim to authority over Saint-Cyprien. The abbey regained its liberty, but the abbot was not Bernard of Tiron.

18. Hugh of Amiens, archbishop of Rouen, *Vita Sancti Adjutoris, Monachi Tironensis* (AASS Apr. 3: 0823F–0825D).

eleventh and twelfth centuries. The form of monasticism established by St. Benedict of Monte Cassino (c. 480–550) had been prevalent since Carolingian times. The Benedictine *Rule* provides for a balance of manual labor and religious offices. The wealthy and celebrated abbey of Cluny, founded in 910 near Mâcon, was the embodiment of institutionalized Benedictine monasticism. Its customs were widely admired and adopted, and through new foundations and annexations of existing foundations through papal bulls, particularly between 1049 and 1109, it provided spiritual leadership for a large network of European abbeys and priories.[19] At Cluny the liturgy of prayer and masses was expanded at the expense of manual labor, in the belief that the prayers and masses of a community of pious monks could atone for the sins of the living and the dead and would afford protection against evil powers.[20] The "lordly grandeur and liturgical splendor" of "life at Cluny"[21] was a generous interpretation of the *Rule* and attracted wealthy patrons, but it engendered a reaction toward austerity and reform. A new type of monk, the hermit (eremite), attacked the wealth of established monasticism and advocated a stricter interpretation of the *Rule*. This reaction between 1050 and 1150, sometimes termed the "Crisis of Cenobitism,"[22] actually led to the foundation of new Benedictine monasteries. This movement toward a more primitive and austere monastic life as a

19. Dominique Iogna-Prat, *Order & Exclusion: Cluny and Christendom Face Heresy, Judaism, and Islam (1000–1150),* trans. Graham Robert Edwards (Ithaca, N.Y.: Cornell University Press, 2002), 28–29 and 55–57, describes Hugh of Semur's abbacy (1049–1109) as a period of expansion and institutionalization of jurisdiction through papal bulls and charters over religious foundations that were members of an informal network known as the *Ecclesia cluniacensis.*

20. C. H. Lawrence discusses the role of assumptions such as that reparation for sin could be made not only by the penance and good works of the sinner but also by the vicarious merit of others, in *Medieval Monasticism: Forms of Religious Life in Western Europe in the Middle Ages,* 3d ed. (Harlow, England: Longman, 2001), 69.

21. Iogna-Prat, *Order & Exclusion,* 30.

22. John van Engen, "The 'Crisis of Cenobitism' Reconsidered: Benedictine Monasticism in the Years 1050–1150," *Speculum* 61 (1986): 269–304.

way to personal salvation, which traced its origins to the lives of the apostles and the desert fathers, emphasized abandonment of material goods and worldly position, trust in Divine Providence, strictest abstinence, continual prayer, contemplation, and withdrawal from the world.[23]

During this period, a number of important reformed monastic and eremitical foundations were established and flourished, among them Vallombrosa (founded eleventh century), Chaise-Dieu (ca. 1050), La Grande Chartreuse (1084), Cîteaux (1098), Fontevraud (1101), Tiron (1108), and Savigny (1112). These reformed monastic foundations placed greater emphasis on manual labor and a simpler liturgy. Often they allowed certain monks to live in seclusion as hermits, and eremitical houses had some hermits living in company with one another, solitary in the sense that as a group they were living apart from secular society.[24] At the same time, the papacy authorized some of the monks to preach because of their holiness of life and willingness to travel. Hermits, who sometimes lived by selling their crafts and were often on the move, also had more local interaction than cloistered monks. While some hermits remained individual, wandering ascetics, others settled down and established stable communities for themselves and their disciples, clearing wastelands and relying on patrons for support.[25] Older monasteries were sometimes hostile toward the new reformed or eremitical houses, but pious laymen who wished to endow religious houses began to support the new austere monasticism.

Bernard of Tiron and His Abbey

Bernard of Tiron fit the profile of a hermit founding a community. As a hermit, he supported himself by woodworking and ironwork, wore rags, and became an itinerant preacher. His first

23. Henrietta Leyser, *Hermits and the New Monasticism: A Study of Religious Communities in Western Europe, 1000–1150* (New York: St. Martin's Press, 1984).

24. Ibid., 19.

25. Ibid., 40.

foundation at Thiron-Brunelles was in a wilderness on land donated by the pious count of Perche. His disciples cleared this wasteland and supported themselves by farming and by selling their crafts. The hostility of the older Cluniac monastery of Saint-Denis of Nogent-le-Rotrou drove him out of the parish to contiguous Thiron-Gardais and gave rise to property disputes. Because his foundation was in a strategic border region, Bernard had to deal with donors who were powerful secular leaders.

Tiron Abbey was founded in Blois near the borders of Normandy and Anjou, with donors on all sides of this troubled region. Bernard was fairly successful in his dealings with the leaders of these power centers. He met Henry I, king of England, and Louis VI, king of France, to obtain royal support for his monastery. He interacted with the local rulers: Adela, countess of Blois and Chartres; Rotrou II, count of Perche; Ralph, count of Fougères; and William IX, duke of Aquitaine. He appeared before Pope Paschal II and the papal curia. He knew the great local bishops: Ivo and Geoffrey of Chartres, Peter II of Poitiers, and Hildebert of Le Mans. He served as prior under the celebrated Abbot Renaud and Abbot Gervais. He disputed the claims of the powerful Abbot Hugh of Cluny to appoint the abbot of Saint-Cyprien and exercise oversight as an archabbot. He enjoyed some successes and suffered a few resounding defeats. Bernard could be confrontational, but he usually walked the corridors of power with humility, often in a hermit's rags.

In its descriptions of Bernard's sojourns in modern western France, the *vita* portrays an era of warfare, banditry, and piracy. Leaders were often corrupt, adulterous, violent, and cruel.[26]

26. Thomas N. Bisson, "Hallucinations of Power: Climates of Fright in the Early Twelfth Century," the Hollister Lecture, delivered on November 5, 2004, at the Twenty-third International Conference of the Charles Homer Haskins Society, Georgetown University, Washington, D.C. Bisson describes the "climates of fright" in five texts written 1090–1130, reflecting the "self-aggrandizing bad lordship" and recourse to "armed power and violence" by aggressive men in search of nobility, throughout twelfth-century Europe and particularly in Normandy after the death of William the Conqueror.

Robert of Bellême was notoriously sadistic; William IX, duke of Aquitaine, was notoriously lecherous; and there were many others whose crimes made Bernard weep when he served as confessor. Implementing the monastic reform movement was difficult when certain lay rulers violently asserted their own authority to counter religious authority, imprisoning bishops and unleashing mobs to disband church councils.[27] Tensions ran high as religious and secular leaders defined their spheres of influence. Even in the cloister, reforming priors endured invective from recalcitrant monks. Abbots purchased their offices and defied the new rules against owning profitable churches. The papacy subordinated independent monasteries that were not decadent to Cluny. The *vita* enables the modern reader to experience the diverse realities of the reform.

The *vita* also portrays an era of natural disasters and serious illness. During the years of famine, Tiron endured great poverty and became a refugee camp and soup kitchen. Those who were desperate for food and shelter were not only the usual vagrant, maimed, and handicapped persons but also people who were ordinarily employed and protected: families, wards and orphans, and local craftsmen. Communities of monks were decimated by sudden fatal illnesses that resembled epidemics. Cîteaux, an austere monastery founded in 1098 in Burgundy near Dijon by St. Robert of Molesme, nearly failed during the famine. It was rescued by St. Bernard of Clairvaux (ca. 1090–1153), who joined the monastery along with thirty friends and relatives (1112–1113),

27. In 1092 Philip I imprisoned Ivo, bishop of Chartres (1090–1115), for refusing to accept his repudiation of his wife and the legitimacy of his second union. In 1100 William IX, duke of Aquitaine, unleashed a violent mob to prevent the papal legates in a church council from excommunicating the French king. In 1112, when Hildebert, bishop of Le Mans and papal legate, delivered the imprisoned Rotrou's directive to his mother, she took the bishop hostage. In 1113 the duke of Aquitaine imprisoned Peter II, bishop of Poitiers, for excommunicating him because of his adulterous liaison. In 1116, when the canons of Chartres elected Geoffrey II of Lèves as Bishop Ivo's successor without consulting their secular overlord, Thibaut, count of Blois and Chartres, ransacked the canons' residences and drove Geoffrey out of town.

and expanded rapidly.[28] Bernard of Tiron himself probably died from ergot poisoning and/or erysipelas, diseases both known as St. Anthony's Fire.[29] Malnutrition and disease made sudden death at any age a realistic expectation in such hard times, heightening concern about the afterlife.

As a reformer, Bernard was deeply concerned about salvation, which he believed was available to all, but granted to few. Bernard's spiritual world was a vivid place. Heaven and Hell were so real that he could describe their delights and torments. He talked with God, saw the Virgin Mary, and struggled with the Devil, whose minions, demons, and phantoms were visible to him. For Bernard, living one's life in a monastery or hermitage, emulating Christ in poverty and humility, was the surest way to achieve salvation. As prior, he disciplined monks who sought security without observing their vows or the rules of the order. He threatened constantly that disobedient monks would die suddenly and go straight to Hell. He preached constantly about personal salvation.

Another of Bernard's concerns was clerical celibacy, which he courageously preached to the hostile clergy of Normandy. He did not, however, buttress his arguments with antifeminism. He

28. Constance Hoffman Berman, *The Cistercian Evolution: The Invention of a Religious Order in Twelfth-Century Europe,* The Middle Ages (Philadelphia: University of Pennsylvania Press, 2000), 6.

29. Ergot poisoning would account for Bernard's preliminary symptoms, collapse resulting from a convulsion, severe illness and loss of appetite, and burning pain. But the evidence points to erysipelas, a group A streptococcal infection of the skin accompanied by fever. The bacteria are transmissible by skin contact and can cause scarlet fever and streptococcal pneumonia. Thus Bernard's physicians isolated him in a small house, not the infirmary, and recommended deep warm baths, which he rejected as a luxury. The death of the young nun a few days after Bernard's death suggests that she contracted a fatal streptococcal infection upon her entry into Tiron Abbey, perhaps from exposure to Bernard during her clothing (§118). According to John Symington, M.D., a specialist in infectious diseases in Washington, D.C., streptococcal pneumonia would have killed a healthy young woman far more swiftly than ergot poisoning. See John Walton et al., eds., *The Oxford Companion to Medicine* (Oxford: Oxford University Press, 1986), 1:360; and Carol Hart, "Forged in St. Anthony's Fire: Drugs for Migraine," *Modern Drug Discovery* 2, no. 2 (1999): 20–21, 23–24, 28, 31.

was an early participant in the increasing cult of the Virgin Mary in the twelfth century, by instituting a daily mass in her honor at his abbey. His veneration of the Mother of God extended to showing respect for women. When he met an attractive lady during his travels, he kept his vows by averting his eyes. At Tiron he was helpful to women, from his overlord, Adela, countess of Blois and Chartres, to his local friend Mary of Nogent-le-Rotrou, who endeared herself to him by her good works. During the famine of 1109–1111 he sheltered whole families, including nursing mothers. On his deathbed, he tried to establish a nunnery. The *vita* emphasizes that women of every condition, including matrons and anchorites, flocked to his funeral. Geoffrey's multiple citations from St. Jerome attributing Paula's abbatial qualities to Bernard are consistent with mid-twelfth-century portrayals in Cistercian literature of Jesus and abbots as nurturing mothers.[30]

Yet Bernard emulated the fathers of the Church in his cardinal virtues of prudence, temperance, fortitude, and justice, as well as in his virtues of zeal, faith, chastity, obedience, perseverance, resistance to demonic temptation, and avoidance of the sin of spiritual sloth. His many spiritual gifts included tears, healing, and prophecy. He was noted for his hospitality, especially to the poor, and was especially successful in obtaining the release of prisoners in fetters. He was venerated for his holiness, dedication, simplicity of life, and work with the poor. At his death, he had no more to leave his impoverished abbey than his body and his promise to plead a case for his monks' prosperity in the heavenly court.

30. Ruth Harwood Cline, "*Mutatis Mutandis:* Literary Borrowing in the *Life of Blessed Bernard of Tiron* by Geoffrey Grossus." Paper delivered on November 4, 2007, at the 26th International Conference of the Charles Homer Haskins Society, Georgetown University, Washington, D.C.

Bernard's Legacy and the Congregation of Tiron

Nonetheless Bernard left a greater legacy in his foresightedness. The *vita* indicates that Bernard made some exceptional decisions about the administrative structure of Tiron. One was to admit artisans and encourage them to produce goods for sale. Another was to place his monastery under the protection of another religious group, the cathedral canons of Chartres, instead of a secular overlord, so that Tiron was protected and affected by the decisions of a corporate religious body. Another decision, made on his deathbed, was to include the lay workers, *illiterati* in the sense that they could not read or understand Latin, in the monastic offices and chapter meetings, so that they appear as witnesses to charters alongside the monks. Bernard was not contemptuous of persons of lower status, and Tiron benefited from the stability afforded by corporate decision making.

Moreover, Bernard's personality left its stamp on the order. Bernard was well educated; Tiron ran a school. Bernard was a trained woodworker and ironsmith; Tiron had craftsmen and workrooms. Bernard encouraged trade as a means of survival; the congregation of Tiron developed along trade routes. Bernard knew many local rulers from his extensive travels who established Tironian priories in Beaujolais, on the Southampton Water, and in Scotland and Wales. Bernard was friendly to women: after his death, Tiron Abbey built houses so that lay women could reside within its walls under the care and protection of the monks. They included Beatrix, countess of Perche, and her daughter Juliana, who were the regents of Perche when Rotrou II was abroad. Tiron Abbey was poor but reformed and structured for growth.

Bernard was succeeded by Hugh, an interim abbot, and by Ralph, abbot of Selkirk, who soon died. William of Poitiers, Ralph's successor at Selkirk, was then recalled to Tiron as abbot. Abbot William (1119–ca. 1160), "a learned and quite religious man," was an excellent administrator with no record of public life.[31] During his tenure Tiron engaged in practices attributed to the Cistercians but not copied from Cîteaux: a centralized administrative structure that evolved into annual general chapters to enforce discipline; landholdings in granges run by a few monks, to avoid economic dependence on the labor of peasants and to improve agricultural efficiency; and entrepreneurship based on international trade that brought much wealth to the abbey. During William's tenure, Tiron established abbeys and priories along the north-south trade routes from Chartres to the navigable Seine and Loire rivers, and along the English Channel from Saint Dogmael, Wales, to Caldey Island, the Isle of Wight, and the Southampton Water.[32] Geoffrey's description of Tiron's one hundred priories in §100 is supported by a papal bull and accurately reflects the expansion of the congregation.

Tiron extended reformed Benedictine monasticism to the British Isles ca. 1114, preceding Cîteaux by fifteen years.[33] When Henry I placed the Welsh church under the authority of the archbishop of Canterbury, he confirmed Tiron's authority over its "priory of Wales" founded by gifts of property from Robert FitzMartin, which was elevated to the abbey of Saint Dogmael in Pembroke.[34] Abbot William obtained Henry I's confirmations of FitzMartin's gifts for the priory around 1119.[35] Another charter dated 1120 (but more likely from the mid-twelfth century) that recounts events at Saint Dogmael's describes a centralized system

31. Robert of Torigni, *Tractatus de immutatione ordinis monachorum* (PL 202:1312A–C and *Recueil des Historiens des Gaules et de la France,* 14:382).

32. Cline, "Congregation of Tiron," 297–391.

33. Louis Julius Lekai, *The Cistercians: Ideals and Reality* (Kent, Ohio: Kent State University Press, 1977), 38. Waverley was settled in 1129 from L'Aumône, a daughter house of Cîteaux, followed by Rievaulx in 1132 and Fountains in 1135.

34. F. G. Cowley, *The Monastic Order in South Wales 1066–1349,* Studies in Welsh History, 1 (Cardiff: University of Wales Press, 1977), 19–20.

35. Copies of the two charters were preserved in the cartulary of Tiron (Merlet, *Cartulaire de Tiron,* 1:41–42, nos. 25 and 26). A copy of the second charter is also preserved in Sheila Himsworth, comp., *Winchester College Muniments* (Chichester: Phillimore, 1984), 2:208, no. 4268a.

of strong government.[36] The Tironian organizational structure resembled that of Cluny, which had downgraded many daughter abbeys to priories in 1100. Although Tiron allowed some of its foundations to be elevated to abbeys, it provided for an annual general chapter to which the daughter abbots and priors were summoned to Tiron at Pentecost. That chapter was responsible for the appointment of abbots and priors and for dealing with disciplinary problems. Abbots of overseas abbeys were allowed to attend every three years. This centralized administrative organization accommodated the congregation's increased holdings and interests and ensured that its abbots and priors were approved by the mother house.

Abbot William was one of the first abbots of the reformed orders to consolidate his holdings into granges run by lay brothers, which he did as early as ca. 1130.[37] Under him, the abbey

36. Merlet, *Cartulaire de Tiron,* 1:49, no. 31. See Berman, *Cistercian Evolution.* Tiron's simpler structure is consistent with Berman's proposal that the Cistercian foundations coalesced gradually into a religious order over the course of at least the first two-thirds of the twelfth century. The *Exordium Cisterciensis Cenobii* and *Carta Caritas,* traditionally dated ca. 1118, create a more sophisticated administrative model, with checks and balances on the authority of the abbot of Cîteaux, and may have been backdated. Berman considers no. 31 to be an "acte-notice," a statement about the history of the abbey and the manner in which it was supposed to be governed, written later in the century and backdated inaccurately to 1120. A royal charter dated September 10, 1121, witnessed by Henry I, given in the presence of Abbot William of Tiron and bearing the seal of Henry I, confirms the abbey's property at the time of the installation of the first abbot, Fulchard, who was chosen by Abbot William and the monks of Tiron (William Dugdale, ed., *Monasticon Anglicanum* [London: Longman, 1823], 4:130, no. 2). The description ca. 1147 of Tiron's administrative structure in the *vita* (§98) is independent confirmation of Tiron's oversight.

37. Giles Constable discusses granges, isolated estates that produced food for the mother house, in *The Reformation of the Twelfth Century* (Cambridge: Cambridge University Press, 1996), 220, nn. 62 and 64, and 221. Prémontré had twenty-six granges in 1138, and fifteen Cistercian granges were established north of the Beauvaisis between 1140 and 1150. Berman (*Cistercian Evolution,* 21) states that the institution of grange agriculture on Cistercian lands cannot be documented earlier than the late 1140s. A Tironian charter dated 1130 refers to a barn at Puerthes (Merlet, *Cartulaire de Tiron,* 1:143, no. 121), and land for granges at Villandon (ibid., 1:152–54, no. 128) and Augerville-la-Rivière (ibid., 1:158, no. 132) was acquired ca. 1130. A papal confirmation by Eugenius III dated May 30, 1147, specifically lists twelve Tironian granges (ibid., 2:61, no. 291).

owned at least one ship that traded in Scotland and Northumberland.[38] By 1132 the financial position of Tiron had greatly improved. During the early twelfth century, then, the congregation of Tiron was an important network of communication between France and the British Isles. Some of its Scottish abbots were statesmen and ran law courts, markets, and an international harbor. Its craftsmen brought needed skills to isolated areas. Tironian monks acquired a reputation as builders, educators, physicians, livestock breeders, and horticulturalists.[39] The Tironian congregation endured over seven centuries, and the *vita* of its founder is a key to its history.[40] Bernard of Tiron merits greater recognition in the study of medieval monasticism.

38. Merlet, *Cartulaire de Tiron,* 1:80–81, no. 60. King David, giving a ship free of cain or rent to Kelso Abbey, officially gave the ship to Tiron Abbey, which supports Tiron's oversight of Kelso. G. W. S. Barrow, "From Queen Margaret to David I. Benedictines and Tironians," *Innes Review* 11 (1960): 36–37, dates this charter ca. 1140 and notes that during the reign of Malcolm IV (1153–1165) the monks of Tiron had it commuted to an annual grant of three merks from the customs of Perth (37, n. 56, refers to *The Acts of Malcolm IV,* no. 223). "In 1267, King Alexander III told his provosts of Perth to pay these three merks to Kelso Abbey as proctors for Tiron, and even as late as 1302 John de Soules, guardian of Scotland on behalf of John Baliol, commanded the sheriff and bailies of Perth to make up two years' arrears of this annual payment." (37, n. 57, refers to *Liber de Calchou,* 310–11, nos. 397, 398.)

39. Cline, "Congregation of Tiron," 449–85, 524–30.

40. Studies of the *vita* include the following articles and books: Jean Von Walter, "Bernard de Thiron par J. von Walter," trans. J. Cahour, *Bulletin de la Commission historique et archéologique de la Mayenne,* 2nd series, 24 (1908): 385–410 and 25 (1909): 17–44; Jacques de Bascher, "La 'Vita' de Saint Bernard d'Abbeville, Abbé de Saint-Cyprien de Poitiers et de Tiron," in *Revue Mabillon* 59 (1975–1980): 411–50; M. Cabanes and J. Y. LaGrange, *Tiron et Molineuf* (Dourdan: H. Vial, 1982); Beck, *Saint-Bernard;* and Denis Guillemin, *Thiron, Abbaye Médievale* (Montrouge, 1999).

Note on the Translation

My translation of the *vita* is based on the version edited by Godefroy Henskens in the *Acta Sanctorum.* The Latin texts of the Sermon, Prayer to Blessed Bernard, and Synopsis of the Life of Holy Bernard, Abbot of Tiron Abbey, are published in Bernard Beck, *Saint-Bernard de Tiron, l'ermite, le moine et le monde* (Cormelles-le-Royal: La Mandragore, 1998). The Latin biblical citations, which Geoffrey quoted from memory, are located in F. P. Dutripon, *Bibliorum Sacrorum Concordantiae* (Hildesheim: Georg Olms, 1986), reprint of *Vulgatae Editionis Bibliorum Sacrorum Concordantiae,* 8th ed. (Paris: Bloud et Barral, 1880); and in Roger Gryson, ed., *Biblia Sacra juxta Vulgatam Versionem* (Stuttgart: Deutsche Bibelgesellschaft, 1969, 1994). The corresponding English citations are taken from the Holy Bible, Revised Standard Version (Iowa Falls, Iowa: World Bible Publishers, 1952, 1946, 1972), and, for the Apocrypha, from Bruce M. Metzger and Roland E. Murphy, eds., *New Oxford Annotated Bible with the Apocryphal/Deuterocanonical Books* (New York: Oxford University Press, 1991, 1994), New Revised Standard Version. Citations from the *Rule (RB)* are taken from Benedict of Monte Cassino, *The Rule of Saint Benedict,* ed. Timothy Fry (Collegeville, Minn.: Liturgical Press, 1981). Citations from St. Jerome's Letter 108 "To Eustochium" are based on the New Advent English translation, http://www.newadvent.org/fathers/3001108.htm.

Chronology of the *Vita*

ca. 1046–1053. Bernard is born at Abbeville.[1] §6.

ca. 1065–1073. Bernard studies until age nineteen as a secular student at an unspecified school. §7.

ca. 1073. Bernard travels south with companions and spends a decade in a monastery famed for its strictness, which the *vita* identifies as Saint-Cyprien of Poitiers. §§9–12.

1073, November 4. Renaud becomes abbot of Saint-Cyprien. §13.

ca. 1080, October. Abbot, identified as Gervais, of Saint-Savin, daughter abbey of Saint-Cyprien, convicted of simony. Bernard, as claustral prior, assumes authority ca. 1082–1096. §§13–16.

1087. Peter II elected bishop of Poitiers.

1095, November 27. Urban II preaches the First Crusade at the Council of Clermont. §16.

1096, July. Council of Nîmes. Urban II authorizes monks to preach.

1096, August–September. Gervais joins the First Crusade. §16.

ca. 1097. Bernard flees to hermit Peter of l'Etoile, to Vital of Savigny's earlier hermit community at Dompierre near Passais, to Saint-Médard, and to the Chausey Island, then builds a cell at Fontaine-Géhard near Châtillon-sur-Colmont before returning to Poitiers. §§19–42, 55.

1. The *vita* is sometimes inaccurate; see text notes for corrections to this chronology. Estimated dates based on cartulary evidence have been assigned to the *vita* chronology.

1099, June 7–July 15. Bernard learns of Gervais's death through prophetic spirit. §16.

1100, May 23. Abbot Renaud dies; Bernard is elected abbot. §44.

1100, November 18. Council of Poitiers: men of William IX, duke of Aquitaine, attack the participants. Prepared to endure martyrdom, Bernard and Robert of Arbrissel excommunicate Philip I, king of the Franks. §48.

1100, November 20. Paschal II subordinates Saint-Cyprien to Cluny. §49.

ca. 1101. Bernard, Robert of Arbrissel, and Vital of Savigny preach in Normandy. §49–54.

ca. 1101. Robert of Arbrissel founds Fontevraud. §82.

ca. 1102. Bernard travels to Rome twice (§§55–58), where the *vita* claims he is restored to his abbacy. §59.

1102–1105. Bernard returns briefly to Chausey Island (§60), then forms a hermit community at Chennedet, which separates from Vital of Savigny's earlier community. §§61–62.

1107. Bernard founds his first monastery at Tiron-Brunelles on land given by Rotrou II, count of Perche. §§63–65, 69–76.

1109. The first mass is said at Tiron's church on Easter Sunday. §69.

ca. 1109. War between Mortagne-au-Perche and Bellême. §§66–68.

1109–1111. During a famine, William II, count of Nevers, sends a gold vase which Bernard's monks sell to buy food. §70.

1112, ca. October–November 4. Rotrou imprisoned by Robert of Bellême. Bernard prophesies Rotrou's release. §§79–80.

1113, May 1. Rotrou acquires the castle of Bellême and gives the monks property and gifts. §81.

1112–1115. Ralph of la Futaye founds Saint-Sulpice-des-Bois and Vital founds Savigny, which later merges with Cîteaux. §82.

1113/1114, February. The Cluniac monks of Saint-Denis of Nogent-le-Rotrou claim tithes and burial fees from Tiron. Bernard refounds his monastery on adjacent land in Thiron-Gardais owned by the cathedral of Chartres. §§77–78. Bernard's holiness brings prosperity to a knight (§85) and his touch heals a child. §86.

1113, May–July. Bernard visits Henry I of England in Normandy; the king gives Tiron fifteen silver marks annually and pays for the construction of a dormitory. §96.

1113–1116. Tiron founds priories in distant regions. §§95, 98.

1114. David, earl of Northumberland, founds a Tironian priory at Selkirk, the future abbey of Kelso in Scotland. §99.

1114. Robert FitzMartin founds the priory in Wales that becomes Saint Dogmael's Abbey in Cemaes, Pembrokeshire. §99.

ca. 1115. A priory is founded in Beaujolais, the future abbey of Joug-Dieu. §§95, 125.

1115. Louis VI gives Tiron Abbey property at Saintry, and Thibaut, count of Blois and Chartres, founds two priories. §97.

1115, December 23. Death of Ivo, bishop of Chartres.

1116, February 25. Death of Robert of Arbrissel.

1116, April 2, Easter Day. Geoffrey II of Lèves consecrated bishop of Chartres.

1116, Wednesday, April 12. Bernard's premonition of death. §105.

1116, Sunday, April 16. Bernard collapses. §105.

1116, Friday, April 21. Bernard receives the viaticum. §§112–115.

1116, Sunday, April 23. Bernard clothes a nun. §§117–118.

1116, Tuesday, April 25. Death of Bernard of Tiron. §§123–124.

1116, Saturday, April 29. Bernard's burial. §§125–126.

1116, May. Hugh succeeds as abbot pro tempore.

ca. 1116, September. Bernard's successor Hugh baptizes a son of Louis VI. §97.

ca. 1117–1118. Ralph, abbot of Selkirk, succeeds Hugh as abbot of Tiron. William of Poitiers, a Tironian monk, becomes abbot of Selkirk.

ca. 1119. William of Poitiers becomes abbot of Tiron.

1120. Abbot William baptizes a son of Louis VI. §97.

1128. Selkirk is refounded as Kelso Abbey.

1147. William II, count of Nevers, abdicates shortly before his death at the monastery of Grande Chartreuse.

1149, January 24. Geoffrey II, bishop of Chartres, dies.

Bernard of Tiron's France

KEY: ■ cities and towns show Bernard of Tiron's travels and sojourns, his distant abbeys, and the towns of his patrons. His distant abbeys are listed below.

■ Beaugency
[Saintry]

■ Beaune
Cîteaux

■ Chauvigny
Etoile

■ Fougères
Savigny
Chennedet
St.-Mars-sur-la-Futaie, St. Médard

■ Issoire
Chaise-Dieu

■ Mâcon
Cluny

■ Mayenne
Passais (Vital's earlier community)
Châtillon-sur-Colmont, Fontaine-Géhard

■ Poitiers
Saint-Cyprien of Poitiers
Saint-Savin
Fontgombaud

■ Villefranche-sur-Saône
Joug-Dieu
Beaujeu

Perche

Paris
FRANCE
0 50 100 150 200 miles
0 50 100 150 200 250 300 kilometers

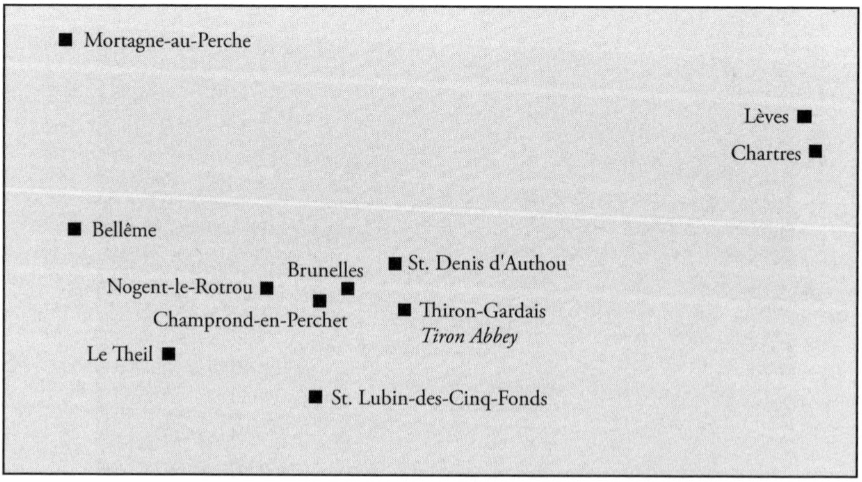
Mortagne-au-Perche
Lèves
Chartres
Bellême
Brunelles
St. Denis d'Authou
Nogent-le-Rotrou
Champrond-en-Perchet
Thiron-Gardais
Tiron Abbey
Le Theil
St. Lubin-des-Cinq-Fonds

THE LIFE OF BLESSED BERNARD OF TIRON

GEOFFREY GROSSUS

The Beginning

Prologue

Greetings to the most Reverend Father, Lord Geoffrey, by grace of God bishop of the cathedral of Chartres and legate of the Holy See,[1] from Geoffrey, least of all monks.

1. Most blessed Father, in your wisdom your eminence knows very well and truly that we are clearly exhorted to transcribe the deeds of holy men and to transmit collections of them in literary works to make their merits known to posterity, by the Archangel Raphael, the healer, who told Tobias: "It is good to conceal the secret of a king, but to acknowledge and reveal the works of God" (Tb 12:7). Jerome,[2] the light of the world, also encourages

1. Geoffrey II of Lèves, bishop of Chartres (January 1116–January 24, 1149), was the brother of Gosselin, seigneur of Lèves, a town 2.8 kilometers (1.7 miles) northeast of Chartres. His disputed election to the bishopric of Chartres required mediation by Robert of Arbrissel and Bernard of Tiron. The cartulary of Chartres cathedral contains a bull issued by Paschal II on April 5, 1116, ordering the clergy and people of Chartres to accept Geoffrey II of Lèves as their duly elected bishop whom Paschal II was returning to them consecrated (E. Lépinois and Lucien Merlet, eds., *Cartulaire de Notre-Dame de Chartres* [Chartres: Garnier, 1862], 1:124–25, no. 36). Geoffrey II was highly esteemed by a succession of popes and by Louis VI. He was an active participant in church councils, papal legate in Aquitaine for many years, and a fighter of heresy and schism alongside St. Bernard of Clairvaux. Geoffrey II was still legate in early 1144, but he had ceased to hold that office by June (*Gallia Christiana* [Paris: Ex Topographia Regia, 1744], 8:1138E). Since Geoffrey refers to historical facts dated as late as 1147, he may have used the title of legate out of courtesy.

2. St. Jerome, ca. 341–420. For translations of the lives of Anthony, Paul of

us to follow his example. After he faithfully translated the Old and New Testament in polished prose, and after he thoughtfully commented upon the Prophets and the Gospel, he portrayed the lives of anchorites, specifically Malchus, Paul, and Hilarion, in a most flowery style.[3] These wellsprings of eloquence, emanating from the lofty peaks of the unfathomable wisdom of God and watering the desert of earthly hearts with the heavenly dew of philosophy, namely Athanasius, Ambrose, Augustine, Gregory, and many other brilliant doctors of the Church of Christ (whose names we have omitted from our pages for reasons of length) encourage us to undertake similar endeavors.[4] After writing countless books in which they fully expound upon the most obscure doctrines and interpretations of Holy Scripture with utmost eloquence and lucidity, and in which, through the reasoning of their irrefutable arguments, they place all intellectual knowledge that is contrary to orthodox doctrine in captivity to the Christian faith, they published floral accounts, not only of the victorious struggles of the martyrs, a spring festival of rose-red flowers, but also of the flowering deeds and continent ways of the confessors and virgins, lilies of chastity emitting most fragrant scents.

2. The corpus of canonical writings and the books of the Old Testament endeavored to depict, through signs, figures, descriptions of shadowy things, the uncertainties of hard questions (1

Thebes, Hilarion, Marchus, Martin of Tours, and Benedict, see Carolinne White, ed. and trans., *Early Christian Lives* (London: Penguin, 1998).

3. Malchus (d. ca. 390). Jerome, *Vita Malchi Monachi Captivi* (AASS Oct. 9: 0064B–0069F). Paul of Thebes, the first hermit, d. ca. 345. *Vita S. Pauli Primi Eremitae* (AASS Jan. 1: 602–7). Hilarion (ca. 291–ca. 371), abbot and monastic pioneer of Palestine. Jerome, *Vita S. Hilarionis* (AASS Oct. 9: 0043E–0059E).

4. Athanasius wrote the life of St. Antony of Egypt (251–356). *Vita S. Antonii Magni Abbatis* (AASS Jan. 2: 120–41). Ambrose wrote the life of Agnes (d. ca. 305), virgin martyr of Rome, *Vita S. Agnetis.* (AASS Jan. 2: 351–54). Augustine of Hippo wrote of St. Marcellinus, martyr of Carthage, *De Sancto Marcellino, Tribuno et Notario Martyre Carthagine in Africa* (AASS Apr. 1: 0539C–0542F), and of the Holy Martyrs of Massyllitana, *De Sanctis Massylitanis Martyribus in Africa* (AASS Apr. 1: 0821B–0821F). Pope Gregory the Great wrote the life of St. Benedict of Monte Cassino, in Book II of his Dialogues (AASS Mar. 3: 0277B–0288B).

Kgs 10:1), and wondrous and intricate descriptions of material works, the as-yet unrevealed lives of all the saints in the New Testament,[5] their ways, deeds, manner of life, labors, sweaty battles, steadfastness in suffering, triumphs in victories, and the triumphal palms of their rewards. God commanded Moses to use as a pattern what he saw on the mountain (Ex 25:40) and to complete diligently all the work of the tent of meeting (Ex 39:32), thereby prefiguring the form of the saints' manner of life, and to make flagons and bowls (Ex 25:29), and a laver (Ex 30:18) for the table, and the cups, capitals, and flowers of the lampstand (Ex 25:31), and the cup like the flower of a lily (1 Kgs 7:26), lamp snuffers (Ex 37:23), and all sorts of things that the Scriptures list specifically one by one (Ex 25:29–40). The Scriptures also describe the Temple of Solomon meticulously, with its measurements, not only the buildings but also all the carvings (1 Kgs 6:32) of the buildings, not omitting the bowls of the pillars or their capitals and the network covering the capitals (2 Chr 4:12), and the axles, rims, spokes, and hubs of the wheels (1 Kgs 7:33). Moreover, the structure like a city to the south (Ez 40:2), seen in spirit by Ezekiel, is depicted so precisely that he does not omit the gravings of palm trees (Ez 40:37) or pass over the immeasurable threshold of the gate (Ez 40:6), all of which, the Apostle[6] attests, were shadows of the things to come (Heb 10:1).

3. That is why the Divine Wisdom, in its providence, which made a distinction between the time of shadow and the time of the things (Heb 10:1) for men of that age, has been inspired to do the same things today, and has willed and ordered the figures and

5. Prefiguration is the belief that the whole Bible teaches about Christ, and events in the Old Testament foreshadow events in the New Testament. St. Augustine of Hippo (354–430) wrote: "The new covenant is presented, in a veiled manner, in the old. For what is the 'Old Testament' but a concealed form of the new? And what is the 'New Testament' but the revelation of the old?" Augustine of Hippo, *The City of God,* trans. Henry Bettenson (London: Pelican Books, 1972; Penguin Classics, 1984), Book XVI, 26, 687.

6. St. Paul.

signs to be described very carefully, for what the wise man does not clearly understand he may learn from the deeds of the saints, through their prefiguration and significance. It wishes and hints that their deeds should be carefully described in literature and disclosed to the future faithful. Since we have complete information about the Divine Will and clearly see that its exhortation imposes an obligation, if we idlers, from idleness, and snorers, from sleepiness, fail to use our pens to describe the acknowledged deeds of the saints of our time and to inscribe them for the future benefit of posterity, will we not give offense and jeopardize our salvation? Since we earnestly desire to make it more likely that we will be saved, let us note in writing the good works of the saints, and by noting them let us proclaim the greatness of Christ, He who is glorious among His saints. When we sing the praises of the soldiers of Christ,[7] we extol the magnificent triumphs of their king, for whatever merits are seen in their spirits are surely due to divine power and strength. As the authors of such literature hold up the example of the just, they will dissuade the souls of their listeners from doing evil; they bring back a sinner from the error of his ways by saving his soul and will cover a multitude of his sins (Jas 5:20).

4. Furthermore, since we see inscriptions of passing things placed on wax[8] statues, and we see sacred miter-bands with boastful praises written in shining golden letters and proposed for future emulation, who among us, considering these things, would not feel embarrassed to conceal by silence the victories of the athletes of Christ?[9] Who would not at least jot down praise of their emperor on small slips, note what battles they fought and won

7. Benedictine monks considered themselves to be soldiers of Christ.

8. Henskens (*Vita,* AASS Apr. 2: 0223E, n. c) notes: "The words *aereis imaginibus* (bronze statues) is found in another of our manuscripts. But Souchet wrote *cereis* (wax) and made a lengthy allusion thereto based on ancient manuscripts."

9. St. Antony of Egypt (251–356) and Eastern monks considered themselves to be athletes of Christ, training and competing in earthly gymnasia for heavenly rewards.

against the powers of the air and the rulers of the world of darkness, and relate them carefully to lift the spirits of the fighters? While we read aloud such texts on the feast days of the saints,[10] who would not see clear as day that we are paying God reverence with the praise that is His due, we are honoring the memory of the saints, we are edifying the minds of the faithful, and we are showing due honor by venerating the saints? At the same time, the minds of the faithless are overwhelmed with grief, persons sunk in unbelief are consumed by envy, and the undisciplined are troubled by anxieties. With all the saints in transports of joy, only the Devil groans, for he realizes that the outcome of all his temptation and trouble is that he finds himself, consumed by bitter sorrow, prostrated beneath the feet of the saints, and bound by the chains of their virtue. Willingly or unwillingly, in his torment and vexation he is compelled to acknowledge their magnificence. Indeed, now the Devil is expelled from the possessed bodies that are his tyrannical realm, for he bellows through lunatics and victims of demonic possession. The Devil undergoes the torture of his own fire and suffers, because he shows most clearly that the saints who are making him suffer are dwelling happily in the house of God and are growing more powerful. Since the saints restore the dead to life and the sick to health, Christian people perceive with utmost certainty that the saints are firmly connected to the source of true life and power.

5. So far, most blessed Father, I have explained, in one way or another, the motives and reasons for writing up the deeds of the saints and have examined them a bit more extensively. I have de-

10 Therefore Geoffrey was thoroughly familiar with the *vitae* of the saints in the Benedictine calendar as they were incorporated into the customs of monasteries that followed the rule of St. Benedict of Aniane. According to Bede K. Lackner, *The Eleventh Century Background of Cîteaux,* Cisterican Studies, 8 (Washington, D.C.: Cistercian Publication Consortium Press, 1972), 139–40, writings about the early hermits contained in *The Sayings of the Fathers* and *The Conferences of Cassian* were also read aloud in monasteries. They probably influenced Geoffrey's descriptions of hermit life in the wilderness. Geoffrey also quotes the works of Augustine, Jerome, Bede, and Peter Damian, which were read and studied in monasteries.

scribed the life of our Father Bernard as you have exhorted me to do (it would be foolish to disobey). I abridged the *vita* to be divided into three volumes,[11] a common layout, but a concise one; so that anyone who is put off by the plainness of the language may at least find relief in the briefness of the text.[12] Since I know that nothing surpasses the truth and accuracy is preferable to polished style, I kept to the level ground of humility as I committed to writing and transmitted to posterity what I saw myself or what I learned from the report of reliable men. Understating rather than overstating the merit of the works, I merely arranged the material from good letter writers.[13] I did not want to obscure the accuracy of the account by purple prose lest the reader look too hard at the stylistic pomp and trappings and disregard the virtues of the holy man. In truth, if anyone, like the infidel Jews, wants signs and measures any of the saints by the number of miracles performed, what will he think of Blessed Mary, the Mother of God, when the Gospels make many other references to her but do not report that she worked any wonders? How will he rate John, the precursor of Christ, when the evangelist confirms openly that John performed no miracles by saying that John did no sign (Jn 10:41)? So it is more reasonable to conclude that many who did signs will be damned on Judgment Day, and only those who pursued works of justice will be chosen for salvation. Therefore we do not commend our Father Bernard for

11. Henskens (*Vita,* AASS Apr. 2: 0223E, n. d) notes: "This distribution of the text is not indicated anywhere. Souchet considers that the first volume might have contained the first seven chapters, with a distribution of chapters identical to our own, the second volume might have contained the remainder of the *vita* and the account of the death, and the third might have contained the Analecta (sundry facts) that we assembled in the last chapter."

12. This assertion may be ironical. The *vita* is an exceptionally long saint's life.

13. In the twelfth century, letters were dictated to a professional letter writer, who would translate them into formal Latin, if necessary, and transcribe them from a wax tablet to parchment. They were intended for public reading and would have required little editing. See Julian Haseldine, "Epistolography," in F. A. C. Mantello and A. G. Rigg, eds., *Medieval Latin: An Introduction and Bibliographical Guide* (Washington, D.C.: The Catholic University of America Press, 1996), 650–58.

working miracles (although they are not wholly lacking), but because we show that he was an imitator of Christ, gentle and lowly in heart (Mt 11:29).[14] So as not to spend more time in preliminaries, let us now commence, full of eloquence, what we have prefaced at such length.

Metrical Headings of the Chapters

6. An excellent student, his conduct was prudent[15]
9. He left friends and house seeking Heaven through vows
11. As a monk, from the start what good things were his part
12. When the page caught on fire, yet the work stayed entire
13. How his priorate's origin occurred at Saint-Savin
14. He did justly acquire the high office of prior
15. An avenger unseen punished one who was mean
16. In what way he took note of one far and remote
17. His mystical sight of a monks' choir one night
18. In what way God's revered loving Mother appeared
19. He fled from preeminence seeking subservience
20. Of hermit life a lover, his name kept under cover
23. A noble speaker made his work a simple trade
25. The way that hastily he made for the high sea
26. His heart with Christ was filled; his coins a pauper thrilled
28. While in his cell he wept, o'er sea a kind storm swept
36. For abbot, Saint-Savin sought out the godly man
38. He saw the young man's turn of mind and said: return

14. These four sentences beginning "In truth" are taken nearly verbatim from Abbot Odo's life of St. Gregory of Tours, *Vita Sancti Gregorii Episcopi Turonensis Per Odonem Abbatem, Prologus* (PL 71:0115).

15. Henskens (*Vita,* AASS Apr. 2: 0223E–F, n. e) believed that these seventy headings in verse were composed by the copyist Jean Pignore de Vallea when he copied the manuscript of Geoffrey Grossus and divided it into seventy chapters. Since Henskens divided the *vita* differently, he grouped the verses together after the Prologue and numbered them to correspond to his new division of 142 paragraphs.

39. In what way he sojourned out at sea and returned
40. A pious delusion fetched him from seclusion
44. The abbot's last direction supported his election
45. With vigilance, his flaws he mastered through set laws
48. The brave man was not cowed by an armed vicious crowd
49. His brother monks he spurned, to the desert he returned
51. Many priests were involved in wedlock he dissolved
55. Why he first left his home on a donkey for Rome
56. How attempts to drive him out made his resolve more stout

In Rome, what was the sense of the man's new defense

59. What powers and scope the man had from the Pope
60. Thieves robbed the saint, to be immersed in dead-calm sea
61. Their workload caused qualms, so he shortened the Psalms
63. An angel urged confidence in ducal benevolence
64. The duke, coaxed to retract, gave them another tract
65. From a lamp he discerned the duke's gift should not be spurned
66. At a hopeless host's request the man found himself a guest
70. The way God bent to him; what food He sent to him
73. A wolf amazingly served him miraculously
75. With discipline restored, from Heaven flowers poured
75. Those he prays for feel showers of snowflakes, dew and flowers
76. Bernard, your prayer repels the flames from nearby cells
77. He fled where a second tract of farmland beckoned
79. Rotrou, his prayers you know saved you from a cruel foe
83. In what manner the key was snatched by the Enemy
84. The Father's prayers appealed for a Brother, who was revealed
85. A poor host's hospitality to a poor man brings prosperity

86. He restored vision loss by the power of the Cross

88. A brother had a spirit malign he drove out with the Cross's sign

He realized in his absence a brother's fiendish torments

89. When he came around, the wheel-crushed boy rose sound

91. A light none bore was spied, the saint's footsteps to guide

94. A silent mouth disclosed a brother ill-disposed

95. The knowledge of Bernard spread widely like fine nard

101. The kind man was no terror when someone fell in error

105. What a horrendous stroke the clay vessel took and broke

107. In what a kindly fashion he soothed weepers through compassion

112. The flock heard from the father the Law means loving, rather

116. He left it to on High if he should live or die

117. How a matron could see him appear marvelously

119. Those who had gone before called the Hero to Heaven's door

122. The dying father bade all keep awake and fight off sleep

123. Relieved of the burden of the flesh, he began to prophesy afresh

125. Amazingly, those far away soon learned he had passed away

126. How many came likewise, who learned of his demise

127. His special meal he got mixed in the common pot,

and his white loaf's stead he chose a coarser bread

He often burned with thirst and yet made no outburst

138. The Brother in temptation's snares was calmed down by the Father's prayers

139. How guilelessly he proved his perspicacity

140. How a fierce nature bent through his wise government

142. He gave with clemency what a pauper took wrongfully

CHAPTER I

Bernard's Education and Monastic Life in the Monastery of Saint-Cyprien

6. Bernard, a native of Ponthieu[1] in the territory of Abbeville, was born to honest and religious parents, who did hospice and humanitarian work and, insofar as their means allowed, diligently ministered to Christ in the form of His poorest members. They designated him for a liberal education, and by heavenly grace he took pleasure in his studies from the cradle. He applied himself easily to all that he was taught, and he was so well educated that he always possessed considerable abilities in grammar and dialectical reasoning and other literary arts. While he was living sensibly among the other young schoolboys, he did not enter into the easy ways (Mt 7:13) of the world but avoided loose living by such hard studying that he fled from the venom of the serpent (Ps 58:4) and the deadly pestilence. While adolescents of his age pursued idle public spectacles, as all in that age group are apt to do, he withdrew into the inner chamber of his own soul, writing or reading or profitably meditating. He sought to avert his eyes so he would not see empty things, for he thirsted for revival in the way of God.

7. At that time his soul was already so inflamed by his love

1. Ponthieu is a region of Picardy between the valleys of the Somme and the Authie.

of religion that he began to dress like a canon regular,[2] and, in keeping with the deportment and comportment of that habit, he lived so soberly and behaved so modestly that many of his fellow schoolboys jeered and called him a monk. Nevertheless the young man preferred to endure their hostile ridicule good-naturedly than to abandon the purity and purpose of a good life and to participate in the deadly deeds of corrupt mankind. Divine Love was already influencing him by its inspiration, so that it strengthened his mind to endure their annoying mockery, separating him from the lost masses, and adorned him with the gifts of holiness. Thus until his twentieth year he mastered the disciplines of scholarship, and he acquired an exceedingly lively and penetrating understanding in his studies of the Scriptures.

8. Day by day he burned with greater and greater longing for the holy life (*RB* 21.1). That fire, which the Son of God came to bring to the earth, was kindled within him from that early age to inflame his mind, and, since that fire blazed higher every day and revealed itself by radiant signs of holiness, it could not be concealed. Indeed, who could conceal a fire? Then it grew stronger and increased so much that it tried to break out into a conflagration with larger flames. When it broke out and further inflamed his soul, it sought to lure him toward the goal of having him totally disregard the emptiness of worldly things and join the followers of the monastic profession. Divine Love acted this way, so that the shoot of the good plant, which it had pruned from love of passing things, would be grafted into the twig of a good tree. Divine Love did not want him to stay longer among his fellow schoolmen, lest their sinful and wicked example deflect his soul from its good purpose.

9. The young man yielded to the holy influences and did not put off what he felt impelled to do. He left his native Ponthieu

2. Canons regular were communities of clergy who renounced private property, observed a monastic schedule and rule, particularly the Rule of Saint Augustine, and shared a dormitory and refectory (Lawrence, *Medieval Monasticism,* 164, 292).

and went to parts of the region of Aquitaine,[3] accompanied by three companions of the same age, who ardently longed to do the same as he. These two-wheeled chariots rolled swiftly toward their objective; they encountered the king of the Franks.[4] Bernard had a premonition and was moved to say to his companions then and there: "Hey, fellows, let's go on eagerly, confident that we will find the heavenly king, whom we are looking for, since we've found the earthly king on our journey, when we weren't looking for him at all." Led by the Lord, they came to Poitiers[5] and stayed there for some time. By careful questioning they tried to find out which monks in Aquitaine most strictly observed the discipline of life under the *Rule*. They inquired so they could join the better ones and entrust their lives to be ruled by the holier ones. The monastery of Saint-Cyprien was located not far from that city, and at that time the abbot ruling it was named Renaud.[6] He was an exceedingly erudite man of letters, gifted with so much wisdom that he was a most eloquent concluding speaker for lawsuits in public assemblies. He was well known and accepted in the Roman curia on that account, and in Aquitaine he was considered a celebrity. Rumor[7] reported to Bernard that Renaud was a disciple of St. Robert, the founder of the monastery called Chaise-Dieu, and that report made Bernard long to listen to Renaud's instruction.[8]

3. Aquitaine was a large duchy extending from Brittany to the Pyrenees.

4. Philip I (r. 1060–1109).

5. Poitiers was the seat of the dukes of Aquitaine.

6. Abbot Renaud (r. November 4, 1073–May 23, 1100), first a teacher and famous scholar, spent his early years as a monk and claustral prior under the direction of St. Robert of Turlande, the founder of Chaise-Dieu (*Gallia Christiana* [Paris: Palmé, 1873], 2:1233–34).

7. The House of Rumor is described in Ovid: "Rumor herself keeps an eye on the entire universe and sees all that happens on land, at sea, and in the sky" (*The Metamorphoses of Ovid*, trans. Michael Simpson [Amherst: University of Massachusetts Press, 2001], Book 12, lines 39–63, 200).

8. Marbod's *vita* of Robert of Turlande, abbot of Chaise-Dieu (b. 1001, d. 1067). *Vita S. Robertus, Abbas Casae-Dei Ordinis Benedictini, in Gallia* (AASS Apr. 3: 0317C–0326A). The Abbey of Chaise-Dieu in Auvergne, Haute-Loire, 24.5 kilometers (14.7 miles) east of Brioude.

10. At that time the above-mentioned monastery had many monks,[9] noble in family, nobler still in holiness of life[10] and great purity of morals. One of them was Hildebert, subsequently abbot of the monastery of Déols[11] and then archbishop of Bourges, to whom the Virgin Mary, the Blessed Mother of God, was moved to appear when he was in tribulation and to bring him consolation. Another was Gervais, subsequently abbot of Saint-Savin, a splendid man distinguished by extreme abstinence and all virtues.[12] There was also Garnier, lord of the castle called Montmorillon.[13] A lover of poverty and solitude, he once abandoned the common life in the community of monks because he wanted to lead a hermit's life. One day, while he was walking through a desert wasteland, he saw a man who was possessed by a demon. Taking pity on his suffering, and calling upon the strength of Jesus Christ by prayer, Garnier cast out the demon that had possessed him and sent him on his way safe and sound. The large monastery of Saint-Cyprien was famous for them and many similar men. Divine Providence wanted to add its servant Bernard to their number, so that, by the addition of a very strong recruit to the stronger soldiers, the whole army would be made bolder and stouter against enemy hosts. So, fortunately, Divine Providence induced him to travel until he came into the presence of the above-mentioned Father Renaud. After the abbot had care-

9. Orderic Vitalis, *Historia ecclesiastica; The Ecclesiastical History of Orderic Vitalis,* ed. and trans. Marjorie Chibnall, Oxford Medieval Texts (Oxford: Clarendon Press, 1969–1980), 4: Book VIII, 27, 327–29; 327, n. 3; and 328, n. 1. Renaud, Gervais, Hildebert/Audebert, and Garnier of Montmorillon were monks of Chaise-Dieu, and the Montmorillon brothers do not appear as witnesses to the charters of Saint-Cyprien. Audebert became abbot of Déols in 1087 and archbishop of Bourges in 1092.

10. Jerome, "Ad Eustochium," 1, CSEL 55:306, no. 108, beginning "noble in family."

11. Déols is a suburb of Châteauroux, Indre.

12. See §14–16 for a less favorable assessment of Gervais.

13. Montmorillon, in Poitou-Charentes, Vienne, is located 44 kilometers (26.4 miles) southeast of Poitiers and 15 kilometers (9 miles) south of Saint-Savin, also on the Gartempe River.

fully fortified Bernard by sufficient instruction and exhortation, he clothed him in the habit of the holy life (*RB* 21:1) and by the distinctive tonsure of a monk added him to the body of members of the community.

11. Once Bernard was admitted to the monastery and instructed by the above-mentioned holy brothers about the institutions and customs of monastic life, he speedily rose to the summit of perfection and was held in universal admiration. What words could express the humility with which he led his life and the subjection to which he submitted? He waited on everybody, he was available to all (RB 53:18) and served each and every one. He heeded all the superiors, respected the elders (RB 4.70), and showed deference to his teachers, obeying all and contradicting none. Loving all unfeignedly, embracing all hearts with tender and merciful sympathy, he shared everyone's suffering, putting the interests of others first and his own last. He envied none, disparaged none, never grumbling (RB 40.8–9), never mumbling, judging none, condemning none; his words always echoed those of Christ: peace, mercy. Whoever knew him to be angry, whoever knew him to be excitable (*RB* 31.1, 64.16)? He was always serene in mind, mild in speech, polished in language, cheerful in cordiality, superior in discretion, an opponent of injustice and of justice a proponent,[14] confident in faith, robust in hope, generous in love (1 Cor 13:13), and, to conclude briefly, distinguished by the purity of his morals. Whoever tamed his body more strictly by the torments of severe abstinence, cold, and vigils?

12. He concentrated fully on reading and meditating on the Scriptures, and so he spent the greater part of the night awake

14. A search for the phrase *justitiae propugnator* in Library of Latin Texts (CLCLT-6) database by the Centre Traditio Litterarum Occidentalium (CTLO) (Turnhout: Brepols, 2006) showed that it was first used by St. Bernard of Clairvaux in a letter to Pope Lucius II (r. March 12, 1144, to February 15, 1145). *S. Bernardi Opera, Epistolae,* eds. Jean Leclercq, Charles H. Talbot, and Henri-Marie Rochais (Rome: Editiones Cistercienses, 1977), 8:481, line 8, no. 520. Most likely Geoffrey borrowed the phrase (repeated in §48) when writing at a later date.

reading the holy books and stayed up even later contemplating the divine plan.[15] One night while he was occupied with his studies, he was overcome by sleep. He had obtained a fairly large candle for that work, and it fell from his limp hand onto the book. He slept, and the candle burned lying on the page until it was entirely consumed, and yet the book of Scripture was not burned.[16] Thus he spent ten years or more in the cloister of Saint-Cyprien in rigorous abstinence. He shone with the radiance of a great many virtues, so that he illuminated the entire community by the rays of his holiness and inspired its members to do better less by words than by deeds. By his words he taught the teachers who had previously instructed him, not by discursive arguments or polished language but by virtue of his works. Thus he began to acquire preeminence within the whole community, not through precedence of place, but through excellence in holiness and the authority of good works.

15. The translation of *divinarum rationum* as divine plan is based on the translation of a citation of Lucretius, *De summa caeli ratione deumque,* in D. P. Simpson, *Cassell's New Latin Dictionary* (New York: Funk & Wagnalls, 1959), 501.

16. St. Maieul of Cluny fell asleep and dropped a burning candle on the page of a book at the abbey of Saint-Denis near Paris, and the book remained intact. Nalgod, *De Sancto Majolo, Abbate Cluniensi in Gallia* (S), 4.37, AASS May 2: 0667A; Syrus and Aldebaldus, *Alia Vita,* 2.54, AASS May 2: 0683D; Odilo, *Vita III,* 2.12, Ibid., 0688D–E.

CHAPTER 2

Claustral Prior of the Monastery of Saint-Savin, Discipline Restored, and Other Splendid Deeds

13. At that time a monk of the monastery of Saint-Cyprien, namely Gervais, whom we mentioned above, was requested by many prayers of the entire community to consent to rule the abbey of Saint-Savin.[1] There was no way Gervais could be induced to consent, neither by the bishop's command nor by the obedience his abbot could demand, unless they would hand over the holy Bernard as his assistant. When at last Gervais won that concession, he was appointed abbot and Bernard was made the prior of the community. Thus by divine counsel two great lights[2] were sent to dispel the darkness of that monastery, because through the negligence of the preceding abbot of Saint-Savin,[3] the community in that place had stopped living according to the *Rule* and had replaced strict discipline with lukewarmness (*RB* 18:25)

1. Saint-Savin, in Poitou-Charentes, Vienne, was a daughter monastery of Saint-Cyprien located at Saint-Savin-sur-Gartempe across the Vienne River, 45.5 kilometers (27.3 miles) east of Poitiers. It was constructed on the site of the martyrdom of two brothers: Savin and Cyprien, in the mid-fifth century. Gervais witnessed a charter as its abbot in 1082.

2. This image of two lights is repeated in §62.

3. Favreau (*Saint-Savin,* 15–16) describes the dissoluteness of Saint-Savin under the unnamed successor (ca. 1050) of Abbot Odo (r. 1010–post 1040), citing Dom Fonteneau (Poitiers: Médiathèque), 80: 434.

and dissolute living. Since Gervais was well aware of it beforehand and was motivated by divine counsel that was good and wise, he did not wish to take sole responsibility, lest he work externally on the administration of their temporalities[4] and neglect to work internally, sustaining their spirituality. Because the two worked together and helped one another, one procuring without, the other providing within, by the grace of God within a short time the monastery was soon restored to such purity of holy life that, while it had been infamous for its impropriety, thereafter it would be famous for its piety.

14. At that time, a serious dispute arose between the much-mentioned Gervais and the venerable Bernard on account of a church, which caused dissension among the monks of their monastery. In order to expand and enrich the monastery, Gervais eagerly persisted in acquiring the celebrated church. Bernard totally resisted acquiring the church, warning that the plague of simony was infiltrating the monastery indirectly. So it occurred, and after Gervais saw he could not prevail in the least, and the abbot of Saint-Cyprien at that time obtained the church he had so coveted, in heated indignation he turned against Bernard, man of God. Gervais disdainfully neglected the responsibilities entrusted to him, and built a dwelling for himself at Saint-Cyprien at Saint-Savin's expense, wherein afterward he lived a long time.[5] We have not gone into this matter in such depth in order to simplify the subtle point[6] causing the dissension, but, as will be set forth sub-

4. Temporalities are the land, real estate, and properties owned by the monastery; income derived from temporalities is used to support members of the community. Lawrence, *Medieval Monasticism,* 302.

5. Churches represented sources of considerable revenue. The parishioners' tithes were collected strictly, and the owner of the church, after using a fraction of the income to pay the salary of a vicar to minister to the spiritual needs of the parishioners, could avail himself of the rest. Saint-Savin owned eighteen churches in 1093 (Favreau, *Saint-Savin,* 18). While permission from the bishop was required after 1078, the purchase was not unprecedented. The unnamed abbot's conviction for simony and flight in 1080 seems to have been attributed to Gervais to explain the tensions between Bernard and him.

6. Literally, quodlibet argument.

sequently, so that we may reveal God-fearing judgments together with mighty instructive works, by transmitting them to posterity. Many are most eager to read that a dispute also arose among them (Lk 22:24), when those people, as the Gospel attests, were visibly complying with the directives of Heaven, rather than to read what is related in the Book of Acts, "The company of those who believed were of one heart and soul" (Acts 4:32). Since we have absolutely no desire to give satisfaction to those with a biased interpretation of Holy Scripture who contrive to misread it with inexplicable duplicity, let us return to where we left off, a topic from which we slightly digressed.

15. Meanwhile Bernard was deprived of the much-mentioned Gervais's protection but was not devoid of divine support. Like a prudent manager, ever mindful of his responsibilities, he devoted himself by turns to the external and internal interests of the whole monastery of Saint-Savin, and the heavier the burden of his responsibilities, the harder he worked. So that virtue would not be diminished by slackness on his part, he resumed frequent correction. Since there cannot be any Abel unvexed by Cain's wickedness (Gn 4:1–16) or any rose not found blooming among thorns, Bernard was harassed by many aggravations and perturbed by frequent disturbances caused by some opponents of canonical institutions who were merely physical inmates of that monastery. One who was more tenacious and audacious in troublemaking than the others flew at Bernard one day using abusive language. As an example, Bernard left vengeance to the one who requires it to be left to Him, saying "Vengeance is mine, and I will repay" (Rom 12:19) and calmly endured the impropriety, but at once divine vengeance, with clear and celebrated justice, punished the troublemaker terribly. While that wretch, healthy and happy, was living with the others in the cloister, he died a sudden and unexpected death and set an example for the others by the finishing touch of his damnation. Since, according to Solomon, when struck by plague, the prudent man will be-

come more prudent (Prv 19:25), the survivors were terrified by such a severe punishment and thereafter manfully girded themselves for stricter observance of the rigor of monastic life. Finally, when the administration of external affairs had been entrusted to competent managers, Bernard, servant of God, devoted himself for a lengthy period of time to inviolate prayer and silence. He achieved such purity of mind that he knew many things by prophetic inspiration which had never been comprehended by human knowledge.

16. In the year of the Incarnation of the Lord 1096, Pope Urban [II][7] of the Romans exhorted Christians to go to Jerusalem, liberate the city from the hands of the heathen, and cleanse the filth from the temple and tomb of the Lord. Christian people accepted the papal exhortation and were so spiritually inspired and moved that not only abbots and monks but also hermits left their monasteries and went to Jerusalem. The above-mentioned Gervais went with them, without making satisfaction for the wrong he had done to Bernard, man of God.[8] Gervais took to the road and traveled toward Jerusalem, but since the way of man is not in himself (Jer. 10:23) he did not reach Jerusalem or return from it. He set out on the road taken previously by the fortunate ones who preceded him and by those who followed his entourage, and he came to the shore he sought. As was considered fulfillment of the vows of all his companions, he reached the plain of Jerusalem. There, undoubtedly with the permission of the One whose judgments are at some times hidden yet at no times unrighteous

7. Urban II (r. 1088 to 1099) called the First Crusade at the synod of Clermont on November 27, 1095. Johannes Dominicus Mansi, *Sacrorum Conciliorum Nova, et Amplissima Collectio,* 9th ed. (Paris: H. Welter, 1775, 1902), 20:824–27. See Jonathan Riley-Smith, *The Crusades: A Short History* (New Haven, Conn.: Yale University Press, 1987), 3–4.

8. Rédet, ed., *Cartulaire de l'Abbaye de Saint-Cyprien de Poitiers,* 3:16, no. 11. Pope Urban II addressed Gervais as dearest son. This letter is dated around 1091 in the cartulary and 1093 in Philippus Jaffé, ed., *Regesta Pontificum Romanorum,* 2nd ed. (Leipzig, 1885), 1:672, Urban II, no. 5494–95. It also appears in PL 151:0369C–0370A, no. 90.

(2 Mc 12:41), a huge and ferocious lion, springing from its lair, killed him and the donkey he rode by tearing them limb from limb. Once this horrendous spectacle was over, with quick steps the lion retreated to mountain caverns and to dens known to itself, leaving the others unharmed but terrified by such an absolutely terrible misfortune.[9] While they so fared in the territory of Jerusalem, Bernard in Aquitaine, located not far from his monastery, knew of it the same day by the spirit. Remembering Gervais compassionately, Bernard summoned a monk from his monastery, which, as we have already said many times, was his responsibility at that time,[10] and told him: "Go and tell William Samuel[11] that, because his paternal uncle Abbot Gervais, together with his donkey, has been killed by a lion in the province of Judea, he should duly inform the brothers of his death and have the passing bell tolled so they can celebrate the funeral with due respect." The monks conducted the customary service, although they did not know how Bernard knew. That very year they learned from those who returned from Jerusalem that Gervais had perished along with his little donkey on the same day that Bernard had reported his death. Bernard disclosed an uncertain incident from afar because he knew of it through the spirit of prophecy.

17. While the monastery entrusted to Bernard was being governed wisely and according to the *Rule,* and full religious renewal was occurring because of him, this kind of divine revelation was vouchsafed to him. It was his custom to remain in the oratory after Compline and stay awake longer in prayer at night. One

9. Malchus witnessed a lioness attack and strangle a servant and his master and drag them into a cave, in Jerome, *De S. Malcho,* 11, AASS Oct. 9: 0066A–B.

10. This statement placing Bernard in the vicinity of Poitiers (when the crusaders reached Jerusalem in June 1099) contradicts the description of Bernard's being recalled to Saint-Cyprien from the wilderness in Brittany (ca. January 1100) four months before Abbot Renaud's death in §44.

11. Members of the same family often entered the same monastery. William Samuel appears in the cartulary of Saint-Cyprien as a donor (Rédet, ed., *Cartulaire de l'Abbaye de Saint-Cyprien de Poitiers,* 3:201, no. 323); a landowner (ibid., 202, no. 324); a monk and a prior (ibid., 259, 260, no. 410).

night, after his prayers, when he was going from the oratory into the dormitory, he saw a multitude of monks in snowy white sitting in chapter. Shaken by this strange vision, he felt impelled to enter the chapter and, after he had humbly requested and received a blessing from them, to sit with them for a while, fully recognizing that it was an act of grace. One of the seated monks, who seemed to be older and higher-ranking than the others, told his companions Bernard's name and office of prior. He said to Bernard, who was listening for an order from him, "Dearly beloved, we were monks of this monastery, and we have permission to visit this holy place, in which we once lived working out our salvation (Phil 2:12). We are duly grateful to you, because you have been guided by Divine Grace, and the community of this monastery has returned to a state of religious observance and holiness, when once it had deviated far from the rule of justice. We charge you to warn the brothers tomorrow that nineteen of them will depart from this life within a brief period of time." When the vision ended, after Bernard told a monk what he had seen, he warned the brothers, so that they could cleanse their consciences through confession and prepare to accept the ending of their lives. One of the ones who was to die declared that Bernard was ranting and reporting something he had dreamt, but he promptly heard a reply of this kind. Bernard said, "So that you may learn by experience that I am not reporting idle dreams, you will die the first of all the brothers, and you cannot live beyond the appointed time." Beginning with him, one by one, by name, Bernard told when each one would fall ill and the day when he would die. The deaths of the brothers ensued in the same order Bernard predicted, and thus what he had seen was proved accurate.

18. In the oratory of this monastery, at night, where as usual Bernard was weeping hard and praying after Compline, before him

In splendor bright, attired in snowy white,
God's Mother, who redeemed the wide world, gleamed.

She said: "You'll have much toil and much turmoil,
Before your prize is joy in Paradise.

But do not be angry about being vexed by the toil and turmoil that I have foretold Divine Providence intends for you, dearest Bernard. Instead accept its wise decisions rejoicingly and joyfully rejoice, and again I will say, rejoice (Phil 4:4), for He who proposed to afflict you temporarily on earth will number you eternally among His saints in the indissoluble writing of His predestination." After she said these words, she vanished.[12] Bernard was uplifted by inestimable joy at the happiness of his fate. Afterward he revealed what he had heard to a senior (*RB* 3.12, 22.7, 23.1),[13] through whom knowledge of the incident came to us.[14]

12. At the funeral of Robert of Turlande, abbot of Chaise-Dieu, the Virgin was seen leading him into Heaven. A daily office in praise of the Virgin was said at Chaise-Dieu. Marbod, *De S. Roberto,* 2.2, AASS Apr. 3: 0323B. Bernard instituted a daily Mass in honor of the Virgin at Tiron (§78).

13. The Latin *senior* is used thirteen times in the *Rule of Saint Benedict.* It is translated as "seniors" in *RB* 3.12, 22.7, 23.1 and as "elders" in *RB* 4.70 and 46.5. Because of the influence of the language of the *Rule* on the Benedictine correspondents, my reading is that Bernard, as prior, related his vision to a monk who was senior in religion to himself in the 1090s and not to a youthful monk who reported it to the correspondent over fifty years later in the 1140s when he had become an old man.

14. It is difficult to say whether the narrator is Geoffrey or a monk of Saint-Savin or Saint-Cyprien. An earlier narrator had a more favorable opinion of Abbot Gervais (§10).

CHAPTER 3

Hermit Life in Solitude in Maine

19. So that the very thing that the Mother of God had predicted to the holy man would be proven true, another trial for him came up immediately. When he learned of the monks' intention to make him their abbot, he went away from them in secrecy. He intended to pursue something he had longed to do for many years, which was to try to live as a hermit and to earn his food for himself by the work of his hands. Not very far from the monastery of Saint-Savin dwelt a man who was a venerable and devout hermit, named Peter of l'Etoile, who was subsequently the founder of the monastery called Fontgombault.[1] Bernard turned to Peter, because he had known the hermit previously as a close friend,[2] and told Peter the reason why he came. Peter received him with great gladness of heart; but since they were in the vicin-

1. *L'Abbaye Notre-Dame de Fontgombault (Indre)* (Lyons: Lescuyer et Fils, 1960), 4, places a community of hermits under the direction of Peter of l'Etoile at the future site of Fontgombault ca. 1080. Fontgombault, in Poitou-Charentes, Vienne, is 15.3 kilometers (9.2 miles) northeast of Saint-Savin.

2. In Latin, *familiaris* can mean "someone who has been received into the community of good deeds of a monastery" (J. F. Niermayer, *Mediae Latinitatis Lexicon Minus* [Leiden: Brill, 1997], 409), so Peter of l'Etoile may have had a more formal affiliation with Saint-Savin. Geoffrey also refers to the large number of psalms in honor of patrons as *psalmi familiaris* (§61). Notwithstanding, Geoffrey uses *familiaris* to describe persons like the beggars at Tiron (§128) and Mary, a matron of Nogent-le-Rotrou (§117), who are friends of Bernard but have no affiliation with the monastery.

ity of the monks, who were occupied with making Bernard their abbot against his will, he could not keep Bernard with him long, although he greatly wished he could. By then Bernard was consumed with longing for the poverty and solitude he desired and greatly dreading that, unless he left promptly, he would be forced to become abbot at the instigation of his abbot or bishop, which would involve the anxieties of pastoral care. So he stubbornly pleaded with Peter to take him away very soon in secrecy and to lead him off to unknown lonely places in the most remote regions. Yielding to Bernard's prayers and entreaties, Peter became his guide for the journey, and he did as Bernard asked.

20. Within the borders of the region of Maine and Brittany at that time there were vast lonely places, where, almost like a Second Egypt, a multitude of hermits, holy men famed for their excellence in religion, flourished living in separate cells. Among them were the leaders and teachers: Robert of Arbrissel,[3] Vital of Mortain,[4] and Ralph of la Futaye,[5] who were subsequently

3. Robert of Arbrissel, Bernard's personal friend and a celebrated hermit preacher, was born in the diocese of Rennes in the middle of the eleventh century and studied in Paris. He taught theology at Angers. Around 1095 Robert withdrew into the forest of Craon and founded the abbey of la Roë in 1096. He was licensed as a preacher by Pope Urban II in 1095 and accumulated many men and women as disciples. Around 1099 he founded the double monastery of Fontevraud, headed by an abbess. He continued an active ministry until his death in 1116. There are two *vitae* of Robert of Arbrissel (ca. 1050–1116), written at the beginning of the twelfth century by Baudri, abbot of Bourgeuil, subsequently archbishop of Dol, and by Andreas, a monk of Fontevraud (AASS Feb. 3: 0603B–0616E). See Bruce L. Venarde, *Robert of Arbrissel, A Medieval Religious Life,* Medieval Texts in Translation (Washington, D.C.: The Catholic University of America Press, 2003), and L. Raison and René Niderst, "Le Mouvement Erémitique dans l'Ouest de la France à la Fin du XIe Siècle et au Début du XIIe," *Annales de Bretagne* 55 (1948): 10–13

4. Vital of Mortain (ca. 1060–1122), founder of Savigny, was born at Tierceville, near Bayeux, and became the chaplain of Robert of Mortain, a natural brother of William the Conqueror. In 1082 he became a member of the chapter of Saint-Evroult and then withdrew into the wilderness. His *vita* was written by Stephen of Fougères (d. 1178), *Vita B. Vitalis Saviniacensis,* in *"Vitae BB. Vitalis et Gaufridi, Primi et Secundi Abbatum Saviniacensium,"* E. P. Sauvage, ed., *Analecta Bollandiana* 1 (1882): 355–90. See Raison and Niderst, "Mouvement Erémitique," 14–16.

5. According to a note in the necrology of Saint-Sulpice, Ralph of la Futaye was a monk at the monastery of Saint-Jouin-de-Marnes. He joined Robert of Arbris-

founders of prominent and populous communities.[6] Through Peter, who knew them previously, Divine Providence carefully added a fourth to their number, so that a strong square would be formed by the fourth added to the three, and that square would later become the foundation of a large wide building (Ez 42:15–20 and 43:16–17). After traveling for many days, Peter of l'Etoile came to the divine Vital, one of the men who were the leaders and teachers of the hermits, as we said previously. First, Peter recommended Bernard to Vital and praised him eloquently. Then Peter asked Vital if he would allow Bernard to live with him, although he thoroughly concealed Bernard's name and the office of prior he had abandoned and said his name was not Bernard but "William." In time past Bernard had forewarned Peter to give him an alias, so that Bernard could pass everywhere for an anonymous and ordinary person.

21. After committing Bernard to Vital's care, Peter returned to Aquitaine. Dom Vital convened the hermits into a single group like a council and announced that "William" wanted to live among them. When the man's wish was disclosed, the hermits consented from love, applauded in fellowship, and eagerly offered their cells. The enthusiasm of their love moved Vital strongly, and, interrupting a quarrel he found pleasing, he decided with the authority of the synod that "William" might go through the woods, observe the huts of all the brothers, and take the one he preferred as his dwelling. Therefore, as was decreed in council, Bernard inspected all the cells, preceded by the flock of hermits. When he proceeded into the depths of the wilderness, he came to the last boundary stone, where he found the dwelling of a brother called Peter. This brother knew nothing about tilling fields or

---

sel in the forest of Craon and was attached to Vital of Mortain. Around 1100 Ralph founded his abbey of Nid-de-Merle in the forest of Rennes. He died August 16, 1129. Raison and Niderst, "Mouvement Erémitique," 16–17.

6. Dom Philibert Schmitz, *Histoire de l'Ordre de Saint Benoît* (Maredsous: Éditions de Maredsous, 1948), 3: 19–20, 105, gives precise dates for these foundations: 1101 for Fontevraud, 1112 for Saint-Sulpice-des-Bois, and 1112–1115 for Savigny.

digging gardens; he obtained daily dishes of food for his table not only from fruit trees but also with the aid of his skill with the lathe. He had also built a tree-bark house for himself, not a large one, against the ruined walls of the church of Saint-Médard,[7] and violent winds had destroyed the greater part of his house. So that the fierce raging winds would not prevail again, in order to partly reinforce what was left of the house by a fairly sturdy structure, he had fastened it with willow ropes to overlying branches of oak trees. Everywhere "William" saw what he wanted in such few possessions, in such perfection of profound and prolonged poverty, and found what he was looking for in such utter contempt for the world. He directly informed the brothers accompanying him that he would remain in that very place and said that he would never go away.

22. When Peter saw his fortune with its riches preferred to those of the others, he carried off his triumph in this kind of competition as if it were a victory, was filled with immense joy, and gloried in it. In transports of joy, he taunted the brotherhood, lauded "William's" judgment, and praised his discernment. Peter approved of "William's" intention, because he loved poverty, and rejected support from more material things. Peter promised solemnly that he would teach "William" the craft of woodworking and would make "William" his heir to the craft of ironwork, if "William" survived him after his death. He was laying up such treasures (Mt 6:19) for those who would come after him. When he had done these things, in joyous elation Peter invited the hermits to dinner. When he searched his pantry, however, he found so little food that if everything were set out there would not be enough for a single portion (*RB* 31:16, 35:12). His situation was not new or unusual, for these familiar concerns were a constant burden because of his state of affairs. He consid-

7. The church of Saint Médard, in Mayenne, is near Saint-Mars-sur-la-Futaie, 16.5 kilometers (9.9 miles) northeast of Fougères on the border of Maine and Brittany, which accounts for the boundary stone.

ered carefully that his table, which was inadequate for one person, would not be enough for many. Knowing how to feed his guests, he quickly seized his baskets and went into the woods surrounding his hall on all sides. Hastily he pulled up thorn hedges and bramble thickets and plundered hazel shrubs and other forest trees for their nuts and fruits. While he was collecting various kinds of fruits in his little baskets, he found a beehive in the hollow of a tree filled with so much wax and honey that you would think that such abundance overflowed from a cornucopia. Marveling at so many strokes of luck, he attributed them to the merits of the traveling monk, whom he had just accepted as a companion, because God had provided so much material for food and light. When he returned home, he loaded the table with the banquet. He set out the extravagantly dripping pieces of honeycomb and brought woodland fruits from various trees and a purée made of their leaves. It would have been a sumptuous feast except that there was no bread, which is the better part of a meal. When this celebration of brotherly happiness came to an end, each hermit returned to his cell.

23. "William" remained with Peter, who taught him the craft of woodworking, as he had promised, and since "William" had a docile mind, he soon surpassed his teacher. "William" was exceedingly capable, and Peter was pleased by his dexterity. Envy and malice receded from the secret places of his heart. Peter, as an old and experienced denizen of the wilderness, obtained food from the fruitful forest trees and from practicing those crafts. "William," however, always stayed at home. As a submissive disciple, performing the duties of a frugal cook, he made wild greens into a purée, which he seasoned with salt on feast days to make it more tender and sweet. After Vespers, when they had eaten such meals once a day, Peter lay down and "William" waited on him. He had indeed learned from a good teacher: "He came not to be served but to serve" (Mt 20:28). Embracing the purpose of hermit life and soon outdoing all the hermits in the rigor of his ab-

stinence, he lived on leaves and greens while he tamed his body by fasting, thirst, vigils, cold, and hard work.

24. He persevered tirelessly in constant prayer and contemplation, to such an extent that, although living in the flesh, in his state of body and mind he seemed to live apart from fleshly things. He did not lack the sacrifice of a contrite heart (Ps 51:17) because of the secrets of his conscience; he did not lack groans; he did not lack the sting of remorse, or spiritual contemplation of the divine; or an unending stream of tears overflowing from his eyes.

Contemptuous of earth, contemplative of Heaven,
His body in wild caverns, his mind in the Heavens,
In forest glens, in wild beasts' lonely dens,
He hides unknown, poor, nameless, and alone,
Yet by heart-light engrossed with Heaven's host,
Known, venerable, illustrious, and great,
He enters Heaven's spacious palaces
Acclaimed by the whole God of Thunder's court.
Thus, risen over the stars in inward vision,
Earth's flowery fields he circles from above,
While picking blooms and tasting healthful fruits,
Fatigue and woe are banished by their flavor
His toil and torment vanish at their savor.
Thus he foretastes sweet joys of sovereign good
But may not see the clear sky's miracles,
Yet marvels at great things in mystic tomes.

25. For three years, while "William" hid with Peter at Saint-Médard, scouts sent by the monks of Saint-Savin searched diligently through the depths of the forests of all Gaul, the ravines of the earth, and the slopes of the mountains, trying everywhere to find Bernard. At last, when they found out where he was, they returned and reported where and with whom he was hiding. The monks were pleased to hear their confirmation of his where-

abouts. At once they earnestly requested sealed orders[8] from his bishop and abbot, so that they could lawfully bring Bernard out of the wilderness and make him their shepherd, as their community requested. Once they had these orders, while they made the necessary preparations for the journey, one of the monks, named Hugh, left the monastery secretly.[9] When he came to Bernard, he burst out in these words: "You are to be excommunicated, if you stay here any longer, unless you agree to rule our monastery, as the bishop and abbot order you to do." Having said this, Hugh reviewed the entire matter in sequence point by point. They had been searching for him three full years and had received orders from the bishop and abbot recalling him and making him abbot. When Bernard heard, he groaned and arranged to flee to the Channel Islands, so that at least the sea would hide someone whom the land could not conceal. Setting out after saying farewell to the brothers, all in tears of woe, he departed.

8. Lackner, *Eleventh-Century Background of Cîteaux,* 122. The council of Rouen ruled in 1072 that every effort should be made to return fugitive and vagrant monks to their monastery, under penalty of excommunication (Mansi, *Sacra Concilia,* 20: 35).

9. The secrecy of Hugh's absence from the monastery of Saint-Savin suggests that this incident is out of place and perhaps fits between §19 and §20, during Bernard's sojourn at Fontgombault. The distance from Saint-Savin to Saint-Mars-sur-la-Futaie is 250.8 kilometers (150 miles). Hugh's lengthy absence would have been noticed and would have been punished if he had traveled to Saint-Médard.

CHAPTER 4

Solitary Life on the Chausey Island. Pirates Corrected

26. A hermit who pitied Bernard's poverty gave one of his companions eighteen coins.[1] Compassionately he let them have this little bit of money so they could pay their travel costs, at least for a few days. When the man of the Lord found out, in high indignation, that the companion was taking money with him, he said: "Either you will not be my companion or you will stop carrying those coins. Do you expect to find Christ poor in those parts we are hurrying toward, when we know that He is rich everywhere? Since Christ is rich, do not fear poverty. Christ will provide you adequately with what you need, if faithfully you seek first his kingdom (Mt 6:33)." When Bernard had said these words, a poor peasant came toward them, and Bernard ordered the coins to be given to him. When the poor man received the money, it made him happy because he had come by the coins easily, whereas it actually made Bernard even happier, because he was completely rid of the coins (Mt 10:9). Therefore both were

1. The coins show that hermits, unlike monks, were allowed to earn and save money and thus to hold private property. John of Ford's life of Wulfric of Haselbury states that the hermit accrued gold, silver, and precious cloths and had a strong chest for valuables. See H. Mayr-Harting, "Functions of a Twelfth-century Recluse," *History* 60 (1975): 337–52, especially 343.

made happy for different reasons.[2] The man with money hurried to his home, the man without money, who did not have the first house where to lay his head (Lk 9:58), did not know where he was going, but, since he trusted in God's goodness and generosity, he began his journey, as he planned. Hurrying to its end, he came to the English Channel, where he learned of an island ten nautical miles away that was a suitable wilderness for hermits, which the ancients named the Chausey Island.[3] He boarded a boat, and when he came to the island, he lived on it for several years.

27. Situated in such a hidden remote place, separated from the clamor and confusion of humankind, and isolated from the sound of all human conversation, Bernard devoted himself entirely to heavenly contemplation. Day and night, constantly in prayer, in contrition of heart, and in floods of tears, he continuously reflected upon the days of old and bore in mind the years of eternity, and he was nourished by his contemplation of the Supreme Good.[4] He did not burn with much desire for earthly food, for he was constantly satisfied by the sweetness of divine contemplation. Many days he stayed in this place without bread or a fire, with no companions. When we[5] asked him, he would refuse to disclose what food he lived on, when his supplies ran

2. St. Maieul, abbot of Cluny, prayed for help in feeding paupers and found seven solidi lying before his eyes. He thought they were a fantasy, but when they proved to be real he distributed them to the poor. Nalgod, *De Sancto Majolo,* 1.7, AASS May 2: 0659F.

3. The Chausey Islands are an archipelago of granite islands and reefs lying off the Cotentin Peninsula in the Bay of Saint Michel between Jersey and Saint-Malo. The largest island, Grande Ile, also called the Chausey Island, is 2 kilometers by 700 meters (1.2 miles by 2,297 feet) at its widest point, and lies 17 kilometers (10.2 miles) offshore Granville and further from Coutances or Mont-Saint-Michel. Beck (*Saint-Bernard,* 138, 254–55) notes that Geoffrey seems unaware that the Chausey Islands, with their stone quarries, belonged to the abbey of Mont-Saint-Michel and that Bernard required permission from Abbot Roger (r. 1085–1106) to live there.

4. The translation of *summum bonum* as *supreme good* is based on the reference to Cicero in Simpson, *Cassell's New Latin Dictionary,* 79.

5. The narrator here may be a member of the hermit community, not Geoffrey.

out, since he hid his virtues as skillfully as a wicked man is apt cunningly to conceal each and every one of his bad deeds.[6] In fact, as some members of his brotherhood discovered afterward, he used uncooked roots of greens for food. While he lived in that place, he did not lack temptation by a demon, which wanted to frighten him and to drive him out of his abodes. The demon inflicted terrifying phantoms on him by its fantastic powers, which the soldier of Christ, armed with the sign of the cross, manfully and faithfully overcame.

28. During those days pirate plunderers came out of Armorican Britain in three armored boats. On the open water of the English Channel they encountered two ships laden with various kinds of merchandise, and in naval combat they attacked the owners, who prepared boldly to defend themselves. The battle was fought bravely on both sides: fiercely by the pirates, who were trying to plunder what was others', and manfully by the merchants, who were trying to defend what was their own. Nonetheless the savage hoard of pirates prevailed. The wretched merchants were captured, wounded, and fettered half-dead to the rowers' seats. Soon the greediness of the savage pirates was surpassed by their homesickness, and they turned back toward Brittany, but contrary winds raised by heavenly Grace drove them off course toward the Chausey Island. Bernard, a lover of compassion and an extender of mercy, overflowed with sympathy at the sight of the captive men with their hands tied behind their backs, lying half-dead in the bilge water, robbed of their money, moaning woefully, and covered with their own blood. The pirates were exultant and jubilant. Since Bernard felt compassion for the other wretches, he heaved heartfelt sighs, and his eyes immediately filled with tears. He shed tears over the pirates, who were losing their souls because of their cruel greed, and he exhorted the merchants to be patient, when they were so severe-

6. This phrase is repeated in §134.

ly afflicted by harsh misfortune. He reproached, menaced, upbraided, and implored the pirates to stop behaving like demons, whom they were imitating by their savagery, to make restitution for the harm they had done to their brothers, and to give satisfaction for those wrongs, in accordance with his humble supplication and gentle request. He counseled the wounded merchants to be imitators of Christ (1 Cor 4:16, 11:1) and to ask God to pardon their persecutors, and, bearing in mind the virtue of wisdom, to love those who were inflicting so much harm upon them. But the wretched merchants, moved by a stronger emotion, wept for the torment they were undergoing, and the viciously cruel plunderers, who were rejoicing in their atrocities, scoffed at the words they heard.

29. After a day had dawned and a night had fallen, approximately, when the winds were blowing in the right direction for the band of pirates, since they cared nothing for the holy man's warnings, they departed. With the plunder they had seized they eagerly set their course for the port of their native lands. Bernard, whose heart was moved by brotherly love, devoted himself to prayer and spent that entire night awake. Speaking devoutly, he called on the Mother of God alone to help him, and then, weeping and lamenting, he called on the other saints of God for help, so that Divine Love would change the pirates' hearts for the good, and they would release their captives and return them free and unhindered with their money restored to their friends and relations. Meanwhile, the Devil, the perpetrator and instigator of all savagery, was not asleep and inflamed his pirate minions to do cruel deeds on the pretext of profit so that later he could bring them to Hell. He started a dispute among the pirates about the division of the booty. Some of them tried to get a larger share of it, and some of them asserted that fair and honest rules should be used to divide it, when they had hardly used such rules to acquire it. Because among evil men there is only rebellion (Prv 17:11), they totally disagreed about the matter, encouraged and persuad-

ed by the Devil. They started striking one another by turns with drawn swords, and there would have been great carnage among the wretches if, by his merit, the holy man had not prevented it through his prayers. All that night Bernard and Zabulus[7] were like two great fighters, standing firmly on the field of battle, bitterly engaged in unending mutual combat. Zabulus strove for them to be lost and Bernard for them to be freed, and each kept fighting for his side and trying to win the victory.

30. Nonetheless, our athlete, growing stronger, redoubled the cadence of his prayers, annihilated his enemy, and granted him no respite. Bernard forced him to withdraw, pursued him in his retreat, and finally drove him off the battlefield. Meanwhile, Bernard troubled the elements by prayer in order to return the wretched merchants to himself, and the vessels and the fierce plunderers. Meanwhile the pirates had reached their chosen port.[8] They were starting to affix the iron prongs of their anchors to the rocks on the shore and were hurrying to put out the gangplanks, to drive in the mooring posts, and to tie up the vessels with the ropes,[9] when suddenly a violent contrary wind arose, raised by Bernard's prayers. The wind filled the sky with clouds and piled up dark clouds, which collided, causing thunderclaps that frightened listeners by their horrible noise. Terrifying thunderbolts fell, preceded by flashes of bright flames, which dazzled their eyes. The entire surface of the sea seemed to be burning and belching flames repeatedly. By the force of the wind the fleet was driven back onto the high seas against the pirates' will. Since the air could hold no more moisture, the dense clouds dissolved in downpours, and such a rainfall occurred that you would believe that the windows of the heavens were suddenly being opened (Gn 7:11) to cause a flood and that the ancient times of

7. Zabulus is the equivalent of *Diabulus,* the Devil.

8. This phrase is repeated in §35.

9. Henskens (*Vita,* AASS Apr. 2: 0231B, n. b) notes: "*Prosnesium,* rope used to moor boats to a post on the shore."

Noah had returned. The elements were so troubled that, from what was happening there, it might have been thought that the entire machine of the convulsing world was returning to primitive chaos. The assailing winds, raging furiously, raised an immense volume of waves like mountains, and in their eddies the vessels were borne to the stars, and then, as the waves crashed, they fell swifter than flying arrows to the depths of the pit.

31. The rowers, however, overcome by the acrid odor of the thunderbolts falling around them, were prostrated on their seats like dead men, straps[10] broken, and when the oars struck the waves they were dragged from the oarlocks. As the ropes were undone, the sailyards tumbled down with their rigging. The sailcloth was shredded by the greedy winds and floated piecemeal in the empty air. Since the mastheads were broken, the pulleys and other corded devices of the pulley blocks fell down. Next, the masts, needing support from the stays, were driven here and there by the tremendous force of the winds, and the keels of the vessels were almost overturned by their gusting. The masts could no longer withstand the raging winds and were torn from their steps. The fragments of the mast poles almost sank the vessels under their weight and rolled down into the waves. At length, water began seeping inside through the open joints of the planks, so rapidly that the vessels seemed less to be on the waves than the waves on the vessels. Last, the rudders were torn from their key structures by the savageness of the storm.[11] Since the vessels could not be steered, poops became prows, and they spun

10. With regard to *stranipisque,* Henskens (*Vita,* AASS Apr. 2: 0231A, n. c) notes: "I read that Souchet prefers *struppis* to *strampis,* and affirms that Vitruvius calls them *strophas* and Cicero *scalmos.* If it is read *strangis,* used in the Old French language and derived from the Germanic *strange, strenge,* it would be a collection of nautical ropes or cables."

11. This passage contains an accurate description of a Breton vessel constructed like a Viking warship with a clinker-built hull of overlapping strakes or planks caulked with animal hair, a sail raised and lowered by pulleys, a mast that could be raised and lowered, oars in oar ports, and iron anchors. See Else Roesdahl, *The Vikings* (London: Penguin Books, 1992), 84–87.

like tops. The ship master himself turned pale. The wretches, despairing of their lives, released the fettered merchants from their chains, humbly begged their pardon for the wrongs they had done to them, and restored the merchants' money, for the ship master considered it of no future use to himself or the others. Since they knew they were in common danger they did not attempt to withhold whatever advice they had to offer.

But what advice, what ideas could these wretches have,
When from all sides the whole earth now grinds them to
bits?

32. For the sake of the company, in their struggles they performed all the usual maneuvers which the honest industrious sailor performs to preserve his life from the furious depths of raging waves. Afterward, when they realized that their efforts were of no avail against the raging deep, completely losing all hope of survival, these double-dealers returned to the way of the heart. Since their tribulation gave them the understanding to hear, they confessed that they had sinned, they confessed that they were criminals, they rent their clothes (Gn 37:30 and elsewhere), they beat their breasts (Lk 23:48), they undertook to go on various pilgrimages, some to be pilgrims to Jerusalem, others to set out for the city of Romulus,[12] since both merit prayers. Many earnestly made binding promises to visit the famous shrine of the Apostle James at the far ends of Galicia.[13] After these vows, since the fierce storm continued notwithstanding, tormented by their intense fear, they began to divulge the sins they had disgracefully committed by confessing them more disgracefully in the hearing of all. Usurping the office of priest, they gave and received penances from one another.[14] Then they gave one another the kiss of

12. The shrines of the Apostles Peter and Paul are in Rome.

13. The shrine of St. James of Compostella is in Galicia, northwestern Spain.

14. Oscar D. Watkins (*A History of Penance, Being a Study of the Authorities* [New York: Burt Franklin, 1961], 2:770–71 and elsewhere) describes the widespread acceptance on the continent of private confession to a priest between ca. 950 and its

peace, so that death might find leagued together in peace those whom the Devil, deviser of dissension, had leagued together long before to wage war upon Christ's faithful. They drew together, holding each other with clasped hands, which they thought was suitably devout, so that those whom cruel greed once leagued together to commit carnage might perish together under the waves.

33. While the pirates prepared to accept death, one of them, who did not want to accept it by any means but who wanted to escape it by any means, drew his own conclusions and said the following. "Oh, brothers, why must we perish? Do as I say, and we will surely live. Don't you remember seeing the holy hermit yesterday on the Chausey Island, whose warnings we scorned, whose words we mocked? Let us solemnly promise with upraised hands and firmly resolve, if the Lord leads us back to him, that we will do whatever he orders. By his merits we will be snatched from the jaws of death, which are already swallowing us." Of one accord they all accepted his proposal as if it were an oracle sent from on high, and in witness to this promise, as their teacher directed, they raised their hands. Soon finding some peace of mind, they burst out with these words: "Oh virtue of the Most High," they said, "whose tremendous power we now know by clearest experience, let us live! Grant us time for improvement and give us a period of indulgence. You could not rightly refuse us, because visibly we are not pirates now but professed followers of the hermit. We are not holding the merchants captive in any way, but, since they are our brothers, we must bear their burdens, fulfilling the law of Christ (Gal 6:2). We are helping them as best we can by fighting against the raging sea, so that they will

---

formal imposition at the Fourth Lateran Council in 1215. Some theologians agreed that laymen could confess to one another in an emergency. Peter Lombard (1100–ca. 1160) said ca. 1157: "Should, however, a priest not be available, confession should be made to a neighbor or companion," in *Sentences,* Book 4, Distinctions, 17, in Philipp W. Rosemann, *Peter Lombard,* Great Medieval Thinkers (Oxford: Oxford University Press, 2004), 164.

not be swallowed up in its depths. As greedy thieves we once coveted their money, but since we are now working under the guidance of the holy hermit minister we are taking care to return it."

34. Almighty God, who had terrified their minds amazingly, saved their lives even more amazingly through the merit of His servant Bernard, whom they had called on with special devotion. The wretches, tormented by the fear of death, had scarcely shouted this and other similar things, when their ships were driven toward the shore of the Chausey Island by a terrifying blast of thunderous wind. The swiftest ships were carried up onto the dry beaches by the power of its impetus; four of them were shipwrecked, and the fifth with its tackle remained undamaged. The pirates and the merchants found themselves and their money on dry land with the fragments of their vessels. When they realized that they had escaped the pit of death, they are said to have wept for joy. They went to look for the holy man, for they had no doubt this escape had been granted to them on account of his holiness, and they all proclaimed his merits and the miracles of divine power in loud voices. In fact, when they found him, although he forbade it, they worshipped him as a godhead. The pirates asked him in tears to allow them to release the merchants to him with their goods, a release he had been unable to achieve the day before through his many supplications. Falling at his feet, the pirates asked him to set a penance for their earlier faults and told him about the pilgrimage vows they had made. In order to fulfill their vows, some of them agreed to be sent away; and some others remained with Bernard in order to emulate his innocent life. The merchants suggested to the holy man that he build a house from the planks of the shipwrecked vessels, and they offered money to bring carpenters to do the work. Although Bernard had stayed on the island for several years, he had no house but had lain hidden in caverns in the rocks or in humble lodges like keepers of vineyards or cucumber fields (Is 1:8).

35. This is the prescient stewardship of your grace (Eph 3:2),

O Christ, this is your strength, this is a kindly change by your strong right hand (Ps 77:10). You wanted the elements to be troubled by the merits of your servant, so that you could convert the souls of greedy men, so that you could free captives from imprisonment in chains, so that you could build a house for your hermit lying hidden in cold rocks, and so that you could reveal his life to the world. For several days they stayed on the island with the holy man, but with food totally lacking they could not sustain themselves on raw roots of greens by imitating him. They longed to leave because they were terribly hungry, but, since they were deterred by the fury of the last sea storm, they did not know what choice to make. Their fierce consuming hunger ordered them to depart; their fear of the raging sea struck terror into their hearts and urged them to remain. They were in dire straits, but they had to choose one of the two alternatives, which were either to grow weak from lack of food or to resume the dangerous sail. Since they lacked the courage to bear excruciating hunger any longer, for they felt its tyranny at that time, they tried to find reliable evidence that they could sail. So they went to Bernard, persuaded by what they had learned by their previous experience that he could rule the wind and sea, to have him control the movement of the elements by his faith and become their guarantor with God that the waves of the sea would be calm until their hope of a favorable run to their chosen port was fulfilled. Seeing the men suffering in danger of death, the holy man, endowed with great faith by Divine Grace, recalled this saying of Christ: "If you have faith as a grain of mustard seed, you will say to this mountain, 'Move from here to there,' and it will move" (Mt 17:20). So he did as they asked and sent them on a peaceful sail back to their own homes.

CHAPTER 5

Blessed Bernard's Return to the Earlier Hermit Community and Then to His First Monastery of Saint-Cyprien

36. Meanwhile the monks of Saint-Savin, who had made every effort to have Bernard rule their monastery, having looked for him everywhere without finding him anywhere, established another man as their shepherd.[1] Peter of l'Etoile learned of it immediately, because he lived in their vicinity. He promptly hurried to the wilderness abode of hermits and, when he came to Dom Vital, asked him where the man he had committed to him could be found. Vital replied that he was hiding on a very remote sea island. Since Peter considered reasonably that he should no longer conceal Bernard's identity, although initially Peter had not told Vital who Bernard was, in the hearing of the assembled brothers he disclosed Bernard's name, expertise in letters, holiness of morals and life, and rejection of preferment. He predicted that Rumor's report of Bernard's reputation in Neustria [Northern Frankland] would be as great as it had been known to be for many years in Aquitaine. He advised them to bring Bernard back from the sea islands, even against his will, if they

1. *Gallia Christiana* 2: 1288, lists Renaud, abbot of Saint-Savin ca. 1128, as the next abbot of record after Gervais. Thus Gervais's successors ca. 1099–1128 are unknown.

wished to profit from the instruction of his orthodox preaching, the wisdom of his life, and the example of his holy way of life. Since the multitude of brothers accepted this statement in spirit and acknowledged that he had spoken truly when they discussed the man among themselves, by common decree they resolved immediately to send messengers to him who undoubtedly could recall him to their community through their solicitude and diligence. Accordingly, they sent Peter of l'Etoile himself, so that Bernard could be induced to return by Peter's love and authority, and they gave Peter a guide for the journey, who is still alive today, named Christian, a man of wondrous integrity and innocence.[2] After the tremendous exertion of the journey and the danger of the crossing, the two men came to Bernard.

37. When Bernard, man of the Lord, saw Peter, who was a very close old friend of his and a very loyal protector when he fled, he was astonished that Peter had made the effort so long a journey entailed. Bursting into tears for joy, Bernard kissed Peter many times and embraced him, revered him as a father, accepted him as a guest, and served him as best he could with humility, humanity, and love. After a conversation about the sweetness of eternal life, in which by turns they took mutual refreshment, Bernard said: "Dearest Father, tell me the state of things in the region of Aquitaine. Are the churches of Christ at peace now in those parts, and are the monasteries maintaining strictness in discipline and religion?" Peter replied that by the grace of God all the followers of Christ were tranquil and happy and were enjoying peace. Finally, he added that the monks of Saint-Savin had chosen an abbot. When Bernard heard, he was gladdened and relieved of the dread that he would be forced to be their abbot, which had once preyed on his mind. Since Peter wanted to carry

2. Christian is the first person mentioned as someone who knew Bernard personally, in his case before 1101, and was alive at the time the *vita* was written ca. 1147. A Christian identified as a servant of the monks of Tiron witnessed a charter ca. 1150 (Merlet, *Cartulaire de Tiron,* 2:79, no. 306). See §138 for a second unnamed monk who was counseled by Bernard and was still alive at the time of writing.

out his mission, he said: "I visited our brothers the hermits, and I brought you their orders to return and not to abandon their fellowship entirely. Truly I cannot put in words how they are waiting for you with great sympathy in their minds and longing in their souls." Bernard, who was completely overflowing with feelings of brotherly love, was immediately moved to make this reply: "I shall do as they ask, for I do not wish to seem to disregard their messenger's authority and their request, although I do not want to abandon the solitude of this remote island." Having completed this mission, Peter returned to Aquitaine.

38. At that time the spirit of prophecy touched the mind of the man of God and illuminated it so that what was absent was perceived as if it were present. Two members of the community of hermits who had accepted Bernard had lived together amicably in the woods for a long time. One of them, named Albert, already advanced in years, tirelessly pursued abstinence and prayer. The younger one, named Adelin, excelled in the virtues of mildness and obedience and, because of his calmness and gentle affability, was held in affection by all who were in his company. By the privilege of his old age, Albert had precedence as teacher; the other hermit was subject to him and customarily obeyed his orders. Since Adelin longed to be molded by the example of Bernard, man of the Lord, and to be instructed by his teaching, Adelin left his teacher and traveled to Bernard's island. Without the support of his beloved disciple, the senior hermit fell into the pit of such great temptation that he became afflicted by tremendous irrational melancholy. He would have hanged himself if several brothers who sensed it had not kept watch in order to protect him from such deadly peril. Meanwhile the man of the Lord knew by the spirit that the disciple was coming to him and the teacher was preparing to commit suicide by hanging. The younger hermit reached the shores of the island, as he wished. Although the holy man accepted him eagerly, he said these words to him: "You have come to us, dearly beloved, and yet you will

stay with us for only a few days, and then you will return to the place from where you fled." Because the young man firmly intended not to leave and to stay with Bernard wherever he went, he did not believe Bernard's words or understand that Bernard had spoken by prophetic spirit. He stayed with Bernard on the high rocks of that island for several days, but he was so stricken by the bitter cold that he went back to the woods to get the clothing he had left there and return a second time. When Adelin came to Albert and saw him consumed by sorrow and at the point of death, watched closely by guards lest he take his own life by the noose, Adelin took pity on his distress and tried to ease his grief. He begged pardon prostrate at Albert's feet and promised never to leave him again. Adelin accepted the sentence of excommunication that the leaders of the hermits whom we[3] mentioned above would impose if he went away from Albert another time. Necessarily detained, just as the man of God had predicted, Adelin could not return. Thus Bernard was revealed to possess the spirit of prophecy.

39. Not long afterward, once Bernard he had taken up his not-very-ostentatious household goods, accompanied by companions,[4] he returned to the woods occupied by the hermits as he had promised. He was received with joy, and with their help he built a cell for himself in the place called Fontaine-Géhard,[5] where he lived with some of his disciples for a considerable time. Since he stayed there for a long time, because a candle could not be hidden under a bushel (Mt 5:15, Mk 4:21), he provided the word of life to all who came, and he strengthened them by the example of his way of life. A large multitude of both hermits and

3. The narrator is the same person as in §20.

4. In contrast to the description in §27 of Bernard's solitude, Bernard has companions at the end of his sojourn on the Chausey Island.

5. Fontaine-Géhard was an important center founded by St. William Firmat ca. 1080 for the hermitages of Lower Maine. It is located 2 kilometers (1.2 mile) from Châtillon-sur-Colmont on the edge of the Forest of Mayenne. See Alphonse Angot, *Dictionnaire historique, topographique et biographique de la Mayenne* (Mayenne: Manutention, 1990), 2:183–84.

people in the vicinity flowed toward him constantly. He was hidden and yet he was not hidden. The more he cast himself down, the more he was lifted up by Christ. By shunning glory, he earned glory, for glory, deserting those who seek it, seeks those who despise it.[6] Men of the world look up to persons who are rich in such privileges. We on the other hand praise those who for the Savior's sake despise them; and strangely deprecating all who keep them, we eulogize those who are unwilling to do so.[7] Thus while preaching to all, instructing all according to their way of life and rank, and teaching individuals according to their spiritual receptivity, Bernard became so highly celebrated in the vicinity that Rumor's account of him reached the ears of the aforementioned Abbot Reginald[8] of Saint-Cyprien, and Bernard's holiness in religion and charisma in preaching were disseminated far and wide.

40. When the abbot learned where Bernard was living from the scouts who had been sent out in advance, he was filled with considerable happiness. He had longed for many years to bring Bernard straight back to his monastery, so Bernard could be there after his death[9] and would be the one to uphold discipline through observance of the rules. The abbot knew that Bernard was a man of wondrous integrity, with great wisdom, and he also knew himself to be decrepit, consumed by illness and old age, and thus he felt certain that he was nearing the end of his life. Taking precautions against Bernard's being called away to rule another monastery because of his obvious merits, unless he recalled him quickly, the diligent[10] abbot came upon Bernard suddenly at his dwelling and brought him back to his monastery with a signed

6. Jerome, "Ad Eustochium," 3, CSEL 55:309, no. 108, beginning "He was hidden."

7. Ibid., 4, CSEL 55:309, no. 108, beginning "Men of the world."

8. This narrator uses the name Reginald, whereas the narrator in §9–11 uses the name Renaud.

9. The phrase *post ipsius excessum* is repeated in §85 and §97.

10. The adjective *impiger,* which means energetic and active as well as diligent, seems to contradict *silicernium* or decrepit.

order by somewhat laudable deceit. After receiving generous hospitality in keeping with the place and time, Reginald said to Bernard: "I am here on urgent business involving our monastery, dearly beloved. Hearing by Rumor of your kindness, on which I congratulate you in a proper fatherly spirit, I did not want to pass through here, I did not want to pass up the opportunity to see you, to greet you, and to commend myself to your most desirable prayers. Since I am carrying a considerable and irrecoverable sum of money, which I acquired in this province through heavenly Grace, I am afraid that in this wooded wilderness it may be stolen from me by fraudulent violence[11] on the part of some unknown thieves. For this reason, if you please, brother, I have no hesitation about pestering you for protection. Since in these parts you are known to be quite famous and lovable, if any robbers are lurking to waylay us, they will not fall on us."

41. Because of this kind of veiled and roundabout language, since Bernard was exceedingly kind and totally unaware of the deceit, he consented. As an escort, not the leader of the journey, he led the Father through the wildernesses to a safe place. When he wanted to return with the companion whom he had chosen for that journey, however, Reginald would not let him go and said to him: "No necessity other than love for you, my son, impelled someone as feeble as we are to go to such remote parts, and no worldly ambition inflicted such exhaustion upon us in our old age. You alone were what I wanted to acquire, dearly beloved. I feared no thieves except the hermits and your disciples. Now, thank God, we have escaped from their hands, now we have no fear that they may tear you away from us by violence, now I possess you securely like a sum of money. I want to enrich our monastery by this magnificent treasure of holiness and wisdom, once lost and now divinely recovered, and not to be ex-

11. The phrase "fraudulent violence" is used by Bede, *In primam partem Samuehelis libri iv,* Capitula Libri Tertii, lines 773–74, in D. Hurst, ed., *Bedae Venerabilis Opera,* Corpus Christianorum, Series Latina (Turnhout: Brepols, 1962), 119, 2, 2:155.

changed at any price. Notwithstanding, dearest son, from now on I ask you to yield to entreaty, and not to be indignant, not to be angry with me, your Father, because I am recalling you almost fraudulently to our community. I am doing so from boundless love, because I knew for certain that, unless I deceived you somehow, I would never remove you from the wilderness that you love only too well."

42. The servant of the Lord saw that he could not steal away from the abbot or return to his disciples anymore, and recalled at the same time that none but He who is ever just can pass judgment, He who, in order to extend it to many, came forth from the bosom of the Father (Jn 1:18) for all of us together. Because of the tenderness of the old man's entreaty and the authority of his order, Bernard replied very sensibly: "I know, Father, I know, and my reluctance to give you my assent verges on the sin of idolatry, but it is dangerous and hard for me to leave those whom I united to myself as disciples so forsaken and nearly orphaned. Accordingly, in your foresight you be the judge and foresee what should be done with them now." The abbot replied, "Have your companion here act as my messenger, return to them, and inform them of what has happened to you. Have him tell them truly that if any of them want to follow you to the monastery, if you find it agreeable, I will provide adequately for their support, one and another." When this was done, after a long journey, they came to the monastery of Saint-Cyprien. The monks, who had not seen Bernard for many years, were happy and thankful to receive him. Since they were astonished at the hairy, bearded man dressed in scraggly, shaggy clothing according to hermit custom, covered with rags, and since they disdained this sort of habit, they discarded it hastily, shaved his beard, and clothed him with their own garments. After a few days, although he was reluctant, they made him prior. By stripping him outwardly, they removed the habit of poverty from him, but they could not draw his heart away from the love of the desert.

43. While great happiness prevailed in that monastery about his return, equally great sadness prevailed in that wilderness about his sudden departure. The monks were rejoicing, because they had found one who was almost lost; the hermits were grieving, because they had lost one who had been taken away. The monks warmly embraced their old companion; the hermits humbly prayed that their new teacher might return to them. The monks acknowledged they were adorned by his presence; the hermits acknowledged they were deprived by his absence. While they were behaving this way, the venerable Bishop Peter ruled the bishopric of the city of Poitiers.[12] This bishop was later exiled for the sake of justice and endured it until his death,[13] and his holiness of life was so wondrous that after his death it was revealed and confirmed by miracles.[14] Reginald sought an audience with the bishop, informed the bishop meticulously of how he had brought this praiseworthy fugitive back from the desert, and carefully intimated how useful Bernard might be to rule the monastery after his death, which was almost at the door. He added as a way of forewarning and forearming the bishop that Bernard must not learn of it lest he leave them by fleeing in secrecy, as he had once stolen away from the monastery of Saint-Savin for that very same reason. The bishop freely gave his assent to everything, so he approved the outcome of the matter subsequently.

12. Peter II of Chauvigny (r. 1087–1115) was a learned, devout, and severe bishop whose personal authority inspired awe and respect. See George T. Beech, "Biography and the Study of 11th Century Society: Bishop Peter II of Poitiers 1087–1115," *Francia* 7 (1979): 101–21. Chauvigny is 23.3 kilometers (13.9 miles) east of Poitiers.

13. William IX, duke of Aquitaine, was excommunicated by Peter II, bishop of Poitiers, ca. 1113, for repudiating his wife and carrying off Dangerosa, countess of Châtellerault. (William of Malmesbury, *Gesta regum Anglorum atque Historia novella recensuit,* ed. William Stubbs, Rolls Series 90 (London: Eyre and Spottiswoode, 1889), Book V, 439, 2:510–11. Peter died in 1115 in the castle of Chauvigny after suffering a year of harsh imprisonment by the duke, who did not induce the bishop to lift his excommunication (Jean Verdon, ed., *La Chronique de Saint-Maixent* [Paris: Belles Lettres, 1979], 184–85).

14. Beech, "Peter II," 119, n. 65, observes that the miracles at the tomb of Bishop Peter II are also described in Richard le Poitevin, *Chronicon,* in *Receuil des Historiens des Gaules et de la France,* 12:412.

CHAPTER 6

He Was Made Abbot of Saint-Cyprien: He Turned from Persecution to Preaching. The Morals of the Clerics Were Reformed

44. When four months had passed, Reginald fell into the grip of a serious illness and took to his bed. Since the day of his death was approaching, the brothers gathered around him. They pleaded with him to deign to designate his successor, through revelation by the Holy Spirit, because he was an extremely learned man, adorned with the privileges of utmost holiness, innocence, and wisdom. Reginald said to them: "Although it is not for me to rule on such a significant and special matter, nonetheless, because I fear your ruin, if you will believe me, as God is my witness, I can say in all conscience that I know of no one holier than Bernard, a religious man restored to you by God a very short time ago, to be the worthy manager of the house." Since they all unanimously agreed to follow the advice of so great a Father, after he had discharged the debt of the human condition, they promptly installed the man he had designated as abbot and, as is customary, proceeded with the consecration of the unwilling and resisting man.

45. After assuming responsibility for pastoral care, Bernard took care to carry it out as worthily as if he were receiving this spiritual order once again, not by the prompting of his own will,

but solely by the decision of the Divine Will. He tried not only to be seen as a teacher, but, since he outranked the others, he tried to outdo them in piety, and he tried to govern himself in all circumstances so that nothing slanderous concocted by Rumor could be heard of him. By its integrity, his life deprived his critics of opportunities, and his sound teaching could not be refuted by those who contradicted him. He was not of the number or kind of persons who lay the heavy burdens of a stricter life on their disciples although they will not touch them at all with their finger (Mt 23:4), but whatever he preached in words he adorned with morals and furnished with examples. Of course he had not come to this burden inexperienced in ruling, so that what from his youth he had learned by diligent training he proposed to others to perform, but not in haste or in hurried confusion. He did not exult because of an abundance of splendid things, or rejoice in his own renown, or aspire to honor, or revel in authority over others in the hidden meditations of his deliberations. He bewailed the honor he had been done and swiftly declined and fled from spoken praise. Many persons make it a habit to confer gifts upon their own trumpeters, and while they are extremely profuse to a few, withhold all help from the many. From this fault he was altogether free. He distributed to each as he knew each had need (Acts 4:35, *RB* 55:20).[1]

46. I am now free to describe at greater length the virtue which was his personal charm, and in setting forth this I call God to witness that I am no flatterer. I add nothing. I exaggerate nothing.[2] As among many jewels the most precious shines most brightly, and as the sun with its beams obscures and puts out the paler fires of the stars, so by his humility (which is the first of Christian graces), he surpassed all others in virtue and influence and, while he was least among all, was greater than all.[3]

1. Jerome, "Ad Eustochium," 16, CSEL 55:327, no. 108, beginning "Many persons."

2. Ibid., 15, CSEL 55:325, no. 108, beginning "I am now free."

3. Ibid., 3, CSEL 55:309, no. 108, beginning "As among many jewels."

For this reason he abased himself, so much so that one who had never seen him, and who on account of his celebrity had desired to see him, would have believed that he saw not him but the lowest of his disciples. When he was surrounded by companies of monks he was always the least remarkable in dress, in speech, in gesture, and in gait.[4] He was slow to speak and quick to hear (Jas 1:19), remembering the precept: Hear, O Israel (Dt 5:1) and be silent (Jb 33:33, Dt 27:9).[5] Therefore he was free to extend hospitality and mercy. Every day he admitted sixty or one hundred or even more clerics to his table, to whom he ministered generously, except for what he benevolently handed out to pilgrims and other paupers who came around. Need I recall his kindness and extreme tranquility of mind to all, even those whom he saw were ever vagrants? Since he recalled that he had authority over faults, not over men, he thought most about what was profitable to others and not to himself.

A fatherly rod to the pious, a supportive staff to the weak, there were no complaints from anyone.

47. He was so strengthened by the virtue of humility that he used to preach that it was the only divine commandment to all those gathered in the open air. *He was pure in thought, exemplary in conduct, discreet in keeping silence, profitable in speech, in sympathy a near neighbor to everyone, in contemplation exalted above all others,*[6] strong in stringent abstinence, restored by riches of instruction, most humble in patient forbearance, upright in firm authority, kind from tenderness, and strict in doing justice. That which among men of the world is counted little or nothing he declared to be in a monastery a crime of the deepest dye,[7] re-

4. Ibid., 15, CSEL 55:325, no. 108, beginning "For this reason."

5. Ibid., 26, CSEL 55:344, no. 108, beginning "He was slow."

6. St. Gregory the Great, *Regula Pastoralis,* 2,1, in PL 77, 0026D–0027A. The translation is from St. Gregory the Great, *Pastoral Care,* ed. Johannes Quaesten, Joseph C. Plumpe, trans. Henry Davis, Ancient Christian Writers, 11 (Westminster, Md.: The Newman Press, 1950), 45.

7. Jerome, "Ad Eustochium," 20, CSEL 55:336, no. 108, beginning "That which among men."

calling in full the divine prophecy: And let him who hears say, "Come" (Rv 22:17). Since he overflowed with love he began to admit all to his community and to bring the poor and lowly to God. Lukewarm and cold monks, more concerned with present things than future life, began to resist him out of spite, claiming that the monastery did not have sufficient resources when it was able to receive a great many.

48. At that same time two cardinals, John and Benedict,[8] acting as a legation of the Holy See, convened a council in the city of Poitiers, attended by one hundred forty Fathers, who had been summoned there. They punished Philip, king of the Franks, with excommunication, because he was committing adultery with the wife of Fulk, count of Anjou.[9] William [IX], duke of Aquitaine, was present, the enemy of all decency and holiness. When the duke was informed of the king's excommunication, since he was afraid he would suffer a similar punishment for exactly similar faults, he flew into a great rage and ordered all the Fathers to be plundered, flogged, and killed. When his officials begin to carry out his orders, the prelates and abbots fled every which way and tried to find safe hiding places in order to save their transitory lives. Bernard and Robert of Arbrissel, who were among those attending the council and were very strong proponents of jus-

8. John of Gubbio, cardinal of Saint-Anastasia, and Benedict, cardinal of Saint-Eudoxius, were appointed papal legates for France by Paschal II.

9. Philip I (r. 1060–1108) repudiated his wife, Bertha of Frisa, in 1092, after twenty years of marriage and the birth of one son, the future Louis VI. Philip formed a union with Bertrada of Montfort, the wife of Fulk, count of Anjou. A major impediment was that both had living spouses. Philip's first son and namesake by Bertrada was born in 1093, and Philip was excommunicated in 1094. In 1096 Philip pretended to break with Bertrada, and Urban II pardoned him. The birth of Philip and Bertrada's second son in 1097 led the cardinals to summon the bishops to Poitiers to renew the king's excommunication. The first excommunication had already strengthened the position of Louis as heir, and the renewal of the excommunication would further weaken Philip's position. For this political reason, William IX, duke of Aquitaine, and the French bishops opposed the excommunication of the king by the papal legates (Orderic Vitalis, *Historia ecclesiastica,* 4: Book VIII, 20, 260–63, and 6: Book XI, 9, 50–55). See Augustin Fliche, *Le Règne de Philippe 1er, Roi de France* (Geneva: Slatkine-Megariotis Reprints, 1975), 36–77.

tice and opponents of all iniquity and injustice, did not move and remained steadfast while others fled in an unseemly manner. They did not refrain from beginning the excommunication, but instead for Christ they were prepared to suffer death or glorious abuse.[10] Although their persecutors did not put them to death, they achieved martyrdom[11] insofar as each one could in this way.

49. Afterward, Bernard established managers for external administration, paid continuous attention to contemplation, prayer, silence, and religious observance, and in great purity of life governed the monastery entrusted to him wisely according to the *Rule.* Nonetheless, the Providence of heavenly Mercy did not want him to stay there longer; for it was inclined to do other things through him and for him. So it allowed him to be so badly persecuted that he abandoned his monastery under duress. The monks of Cluny, who asserted that the monastery of Saint-Cyprien should be subject to their authority, went to Pope Paschal [II], the Supreme Pontiff of the Romans at that time, and urged him to prohibit Bernard from holding the office of abbot unless he would subject himself and the monastery to their laws. When Bernard heard the prohibition imposed on pain of separation, he accepted one part of the separation quite willingly, which was to abandon the honor of the abbacy, but he refused to accept the other part, because he feared that the monastery, which he had accepted free, would be placed in subjection. Also, he dreaded opposing the authority of the Cluniacs, who constantly said they were in the right. He did

10. This passage is borrowed directly from the Chronicle of Hugh of Flavigny (ca. 1103), also known as the Chronicle of Verdun, under the year 1100 (Hugh of Flavigny, *Chronicon Hugonis,* Book 2, under the year 1100, in *Monumenta Germaniae Historica, Scriptores,* ed. Georgius Heinricus Pertz [Hanover: Brepols, 1848; Stuttgart: Anton Hiersemann, 1992] 8:493). The names of Bernard and Robert are substituted for the original reference to the papal legates as pillars of Christ who remained in their places.

11. William of Malmesbury (1095–ca. 1143) (*Gesta regum Anglorum,* Book V, 439, 90.2:510–11) describes the willingness of Bishop Peter II to endure martyrdom for excommunicating William IX, duke of Aquitaine, ca. 1113.

not hesitate to take what he believed would be the safest course of action, for, burning with love of poverty and solitude, he returned to the remoteness of the desert from which he had been torn by fraudulent violence and found his heart, which had remained there.[12] He joined Dom Robert of Arbrissel and Vital of Mortain,[13] whom we mentioned previously.

50. They traveled barefoot through the regions of Gaul. They preached the word of God in towns, castles, and cities, uprooting men from the errors of their lives. Like strong solid battering rams, aided by divine power, they demolished the walls of faithlessness and the attacks of vices. They plucked the love of passing things from the hearts of men. They destroyed their evil talk, which corrupted good morals. They despoiled the evil works of wickedness. They demolished the growing pile of all kinds of injustice. They planted virtues, which spring from God, by sowing them in the hearts of men, and they encouraged vigorous plants by their example. Although they did not raise the dead, what they were doing was greater, because they raised souls dead to sin to true life and united them with God. As they did these signs, they toured various provinces, sometimes together and at other times separately, and, by the craft of the Devil, they had no lack of troubles. While Bernard preached through the coastal parts of Normandy, he sowed the word of God, spared no one, and did not refrain from telling the truth for love or fear of anyone.

51. At that time, long ago, it was customary throughout Normandy for priests to take wives publicly, to celebrate weddings, and to sire sons and daughters to whom, when they died, they left their churches by hereditary right. When their daughters married, many times, if they had no other possessions, they gave

12. See §40.

13. Vital was licensed to leave the diocese of Avranches by Bishop Turgasius, who was not installed before 1094. See *Vita Vitalis,* Book 2, 13, in *Analecta Bollandiana,* 1:381, n. 1. He was probably licensed to preach at the same time as Robert of Arbrissel by Pope Urban II in 1095 and conducted many preaching tours in Normandy, Brittany, and England.

the church as a dowry. Worse, when priests took wives, before joining with them they used to swear in the presence of their relatives that they would never leave them. By doing so, they bound themselves by oath never to stop being fornicators, never to approach the body and blood of Christ except as unworthy criminals, and, by approaching the sacraments unworthily, to eat and drink judgment on themselves (1 Cor 11:29). Bernard, servant of God, argued forcefully against this fatal custom in gatherings of priests and tried to get them to abandon it.[14] He drew some of the priests away from it, but he was not able to draw most of them away from this pit of death. The priests' wives were afraid of separation and, with their supporters, tried to kill him, and the priests themselves arranged for him to be waylaid in order to frighten him and deter him from preaching.

52. One day in Coutances, a city on the coast of Normandy, when Bernard was preaching publicly to the people, an archdeacon who had a wife and children came with a large entourage of priests and clerics and asked why Bernard, who was a monk and dead to the world, sought to preach to the living?[15] Surrounded, in the presence of all the people, Bernard gave this explanation. "Dearest brother, haven't you read in the Scriptures of God that Samson, who was so strong, slew his enemies with the jawbone of a dead ass (Jgs 15:15)?" While the people listened, he took that opportunity to explain that chapter of Scripture in self-defense.[16] "Samson," he began, "who is interpreted as the sun, signifies

14. See Anne Llewellyn Barstow, *Married Priests and the Reforming Papacy: The Eleventh-Century Debates,* Texts and Studies in Religion, 12 (New York: Edwin Mellen Press, 1982).

15. Urban II decided that monks might preach, at the Council of Nîmes in July 1096 (Mansi, *Sacra Concilia,* 20:934–35). The dating suggests that the preaching tour occurred ca. 1096–1101, prior to Bernard's trip to Rome and licensing to preach.

16. The imagery of the sermon reflects familiarity with the opening of Sermon 60 by Peter Damian (1007–1072) entitled *"In Natali Virginum Sermo Secundus."* See Peter Damian, *Sancti Petri Damiani Sermones,* Corpus Christianorum, Continuatio Medievalis, Series Latina, 57 (Turnhout, 1983), 413–14.

Christ, the sun of justice. His enemies are demons, and sinful men who consort with demons out of malice, while they oppose Christ and His law. The dead ass signifies simple obedient people who bear the easy yoke of Christ and his light burden (Mt 11:30) and follow the ways of humility, dead to the world, that is, mortified by sins and vices, as Scripture says: For you have died, and your life is hid with Christ in God (Col 3:3).

53. "The jawbone, of strong bone, is harder than soft flesh, and, as the implement for biting and chewing in the ass's head, it signifies the preacher of the Church. The preacher must have the strength of bone, because he must firmly resist sin and vice and bear hardship bravely in the defense of justice and holiness. The preacher must be harder than the soft flesh, because through harder abstinence he must remove carnal delight in pleasure from his existence and way of life and must not weakly allow his mind to be enslaved by softening vices. The preacher is the instrument for chewing, if he understands every bit of the word of God (which is the food of our souls, as the Lord says in the Gospel: Man shall not live by bread alone, but by every word that proceeds from the mouth of God [Mt 4:4]), and, when he understands it, he practices what he preaches. If he teaches well and lives ill, he does not instruct the people but corrupts them. As long as he lives ill, his preaching is disdained and not retained, and his example to the people is destructive, not instructive. So he should live well, and he must break down the Scriptures to bits by chewing and grinding the food of the soul. He must distinguish the historical information from the allegory, divide the allegory from the tropology, and separate the tropology from the anagogy.[17] After he has chewed and ground the food of the word of God to bits, he must first swallow it down smoothly, savoring the deliciousness of its

17. Allegory is the abstract or spiritual meaning of historical information in the biblical text. Tropology is the moral interpretation of biblical text. Anagogy is an interpretation of biblical text that seeks hidden meanings regarding future life. Bernard's fourfold analysis of Scripture was an advanced technique used at universities a century later.

flavor, and next he must convey it to the body of the dead ass, that is to say, to the capacity for understanding of simple people who themselves are mortified. By using all these means of understanding, he strives to tell them how to attain eternal life, since by teaching through diligent preaching, ordered with discretion and wisdom, he improves their actions and way of life. He must not forget that he himself is an implement for biting. He tears sinners away from the body of the Devil by the bite of correction and rebuke and restores them justified through penitent laments to the body of Christ, which is the Church. Just as by the dignity of the priesthood he is in the upper part of the ass, that is, the head, so he is above the people, who are understood to be the ass, because of his good works and holy way of life.

54. "Thus you see, dearest brother, by the authority of Holy Scripture, that if the Christian people, who are understood to be the dead ass, should be dead to the world, how much more so should be their preacher, who is symbolized by the jawbone. He should be crucified with Christ (Gal 2:20) and dead to the world; as that true preacher to the world said of himself, "I have been crucified with Christ." By the authority conferred by his mortification he may punish those who are still living in their sins and vices, and make those whom he punishes be like him in death, so that what the Apostle said may be fulfilled: Be imitators of me, as I am of Christ (1 Cor 11:1). Since a preacher of the Church should be dead to the world, and since his preaching is disdained by people who believe that his life is not yet mortified on account of his sins and vices, for what reason can you prohibit me from preaching, because I am a monk and dead to the world, when I can inspire the people by the example of my mortified life and I can improve them by my instructive words? Since it is established that Blessed Gregory and Martin[18] and many

18. Bernard is referring to the *vitae* of Blessed Gregory (possibly Gregory of Nazianzus, a monk bishop who preached famous sermons on the Trinity, or perhaps Gregory the Great) and Martin of Tours for examples of monks who preached.

other holy monks, by the merit of their mortification, accepted the pastoral rule of churches and the office of preaching together with the honors of the priesthood, it follows that a license to preach is acquired through the virtue of mortification. As for the right to preach, my being a monk and dead to the world does not deter me, but rather confers it on me." Since the man of God continued to speak in this way and other ways, and since he was acclaimed by the people, at a nod (2 Mc 8:18) from God the archdeacon rid his soul of fierceness and arrogance for a moderately long time and prevented the priests and their wives from doing Bernard harm. Such a crowd had gathered for the solemnity of Pentecost to take part in proper processions[19] to the cathedral, as was the local custom, that the place was scarcely large enough to hold them all. Bernard, soldier of Christ, continued to preach to the people and patiently endured fighting without and fear within (2 Cor 7:5).

19. These religious processions, known as *pardons,* are still held in Normandy and Brittany.

CHAPTER 7

Two Trips to Rome in Defense of the Abbey. The Abbey Was Relinquished. Disciples Were Collected Elsewhere

55. Meanwhile, for about four years the monks of Saint-Cyprien had expended much effort and expense trying to free their monastery from the false claim of the Cluniacs and had been unsuccessful. Since their need was urgent, in distress they were forced to go into the desert with letters from the bishop of Poitiers. They located their abbot and asked him to help the persons who were toiling in their monastery. Impelled by compassion and compelled by the order of his bishop, Bernard returned to Saint-Cyprien and spent a few days there. Urged by the bishop and monks, accompanied by a few hermit brothers from the desert, riding on a donkey, wearing his garments of poverty, that is, of hermit life, he set out for Rome with this humble entourage. When he arrived there after much exertion, he went to his lord, Pope Paschal [II], and asked the pontiff why he had deprived him of the office of abbot. The pope received Bernard kindly, because he had heard much of Bernard's holiness from his cardinals, John and Benedict, who had known Bernard previously in Aquitaine and had seen him remain steadfast in the council during the excommunication of the king. Taking Bernard's hand, the pope led him to the chapel, and in privacy he

conversed with Bernard alone for a great part of the day. Then he led Bernard back to the palace and kindly restored the office that he had forbidden Bernard to hold, in a public audience.[1] After Bernard had received a papal blessing, he returned to Poitiers and held his monastery for several years in peace.

56. The monks were compelled by his instructions to exchange lukewarmness in living (*RB* 18:25) for rigor in discipline, and a dissolute way of life for stricter observance of the provisions of the *Rule.* Once they perceived that their customary rule-breaking was not allowed and were unwilling to change, they tried to find some means of driving him out of the monastery. Stealthily they stole and hid the greater part of the wheat and wine from his household, so he would not have the wherewithal to feed those paupers, in whose refreshment he took such delight. They hoped that, once he was worn out from procuring provisions, he would return to the solitude of the desert. But no wisdom, no understanding, no counsel can avail against the Lord (Prv 21:30). While they tried to confine him to narrow domestic concerns, they restored his abundance through greater wealth. At that very time a canon, who knew Bernard was an exceedingly compassionate provider for the poor, gave him so much wheat and wine that he believed it would last until the end of the year. Divine Providence restored to him that very year the wheat and wine that the monks had hidden, but first, to their misfortune, it imposed an avenging death penalty on them. Their supporters had no fear of dying themselves and, unable to drive away the holy man by this means, sought another. They informed the Cluniac monks and solemnly promised to lend their assistance in subjecting the monastery of Saint-Cyprien to their laws, for if it were, they had no doubt that Bernard would leave the mon-

1. Although this narrator has detailed knowledge of the internal politics of Saint-Cyprien and the Roman curia, his assertion that Paschal II restored Bernard to his abbacy is not supported by the abbey's cartulary and seems improbable, for the pope's powerful chamberlain had ties to Cluny.

astery. Encouraged by the suggestion, the Cluniacs went to the pope a second time and pressed again to have Bernard suspended from the office of abbot unless he would subject the monastery to them.

57. Bernard resumed the work anew, so as not to succumb to the blows of a harsher fortune. He was afraid that he would sin if through sloth and negligence on his part, he allowed the liberty of his monastery of Saint-Cyprien to slip away. He came to Rome a second time and asked the pope to investigate the cases of both parties carefully and hand down a lawful judgment. The pope avoided doing so and ordered Bernard either to subject the monastery to the Cluniacs or never to hold office in that abbey. After the man of God knew for certain that he would obtain nothing in the Roman curia and would not dissuade the pope from his deliberate decree, he was forced to call for a hearing in the higher court, where he clearly saw that he ought to turn, although the judges would not be mortal men. Inflamed by zeal for justice, as he followed the proverb of Solomon: The righteous man is as bold as a lion (Prv 28:1) and shall be without dread, not with bold presumption but with sincere high-mindedness, Bernard resolutely summoned the pope and all those involved in this matter to an examination at the Last Judgment before a judge who would be undeceived by dark ignorance and uncorrupted by gifts. When the pope heard him speak so freely, in indignation he ordered the man of God to leave his presence. Then he asked his advisers what he should do about this matter. They replied unanimously that, because the man was so holy, having this controversial case judged before the judge of all would be unsafe, and they refused absolutely to be part of anything against him. In view of the consensus, they added that it would be just to restore his dignity to him and to ask pardon for his exertion and unjust treatment. Two cardinals who were present, John and Benedict, were magnificent public criers of his virtue, which they had known of in Aquitaine, and proclaimed it in the pope's hear-

ing. They praised him to the Romans for his virtue, which they themselves had observed at the Council of Poitiers, where he was prepared to suffer martyrdom for justice.

58. After the pope learned of the man's great perfection, he had a change of heart and felt no more indignation, and he ordered Bernard to return to the council. When Bernard came in, the pope called for silence, in order to allow him to speak for himself and to be heard freely by all. The man of the Lord began: "Most reverend pope, I entreat your eminence in your excellence to allow me briefly to say a few words that reflect the truth. For years past, you, Father, and many who are members of this sacred college, very honorable men because of their meritorious wisdom and lives, have been aware that the abbey of Saint-Cyprien, entrusted to the rule of our insignificant self, has enjoyed its freedom over the course of many years. It reflowered with great piety, before the monastery began to be Cluniac. Now, the abbot of Cluny, according to the prophecy of Isaiah, keeps neighing after my wife (Jer 5:8). As if he were an archabbot, with arrogant tyranny he hotly desires to rule me, an ordinary abbot, and is trying to make our abbey serve him like a maidservant and be his to rule and command. This kind of ambition is novel and unusual. It springs from vice, and unless its stalk is cut off at its root, it will propagate fruits of great virulence and broadcast seeds of immense corruption, if it is allowed to grow. I have no doubt, of course, that this detestable evil, which I call novel and insolent, will be uprooted in its egregiousness by the censure of your judgment. We read in divine compilations about archbishops, archpriests, and archdeacons, but we do not find the title of archabbot in them. The *Rule of Saint Benedict* (which I, who am accused, profess, and he, my accuser, professes) establishes that the abbot alone has the right to dispose of all things in his monastery (*RB* 65:11–12). Benedict makes no mention whatsoever of any archabbot, for Benedict believed that no one in the world ever longed or would long for

such arrogant vanity.[2] I came to show that his malicious claim is false, if I am given an opportunity to defend the ancestral liberty of our monastery, most excellent Father. I came more confidently into the presence of the Roman curia inasmuch as I knew the more certainly that, once our grounds are examined, he cannot possibly get that earlier decision and injustice to stand. I am acting as the messenger of our monastery, and in my insignificance I humbly request your majesty in your sublime excellence, where the most eminent part of the body of Christ is located, which is the Church, to follow custom and to impose the rule of the head on the other lower members. Doing so will preserve the whole bodily structure in peace, according to the rules of justice, repaying every man (Mt 16:27) what is solely his own. May your excellency suffer with the suffering member (1 Cor 12:26), as you carefully deliberate the cases of both parties; and may you judge with right judgment (Jn 7:24, 5:30), considering not the advantage of any temporary accommodation but instead the unending consequences of eternal retribution."

59. Having concluded brilliantly, the holy man fell silent. The pope ordered the defenders of the case of the Cluniac monks to speak. Since they did not have truthful arguments that would prove that the monastery of Saint-Cyprien should be subject to their laws and could not devise any, they began to fashion veiled ambiguous comments abounding in ambitions and roundabout ways of speaking. Since the assembly present recognized that they were totally deviating from the rules of justice, the monastery of Saint-Cyprien was given its freedom from them. When the pope confirmed the judgment, he restored to the holy man the abbacy he had forbidden him to hold. With much entreaty he tried to have Bernard accept the dignity of cardinal-priest from him and remain with him to handle the business of the cases before the Roman Church. Since Bernard longed to sat-

2. Bernard's view on the independence of Benedictine monasteries would evolve; see §98.

isfy his desire for continuous contemplation in the solitude of the desert, he was afraid to agree to become involved in foreign concerns and would not consent to the request. He asked to be allowed to leave the monastery that he was ruling and to return to the wilderness, which he finally achieved with difficulty after much pleading. Since the pope could not retain with him a man of such constancy and such holiness, who desired nothing in the world, nothing except seeking God alone, he imposed this office on Bernard: Bernard was to preach to the people, hear confessions, impose penances, baptize, tour regions, and solicitously fulfill all functions of a preacher to the public. Subsequently the pope gave this kind of apostolic remuneration to Bernard, since he did not wish the apostolic vicar whom he was sending out to preach without pay to have no livelihood: he decreed that Bernard might accept bodily food from those whom he restored by his saving word. Wishing to begin with himself, the pope invited Bernard to dinner and, as long as he stayed in Rome, had him eat at his table every day.

60. Bernard departed after he had received a papal blessing and returned to Poitiers. When he left the monastery a few days later, longing soulfully to pursue the life of a hermit, he went with a few disciples to the Chausey Island (because it was remote from all). Although he wanted to stay there a long time, he could not do so.[3] A multitude of plundering pirates landed on the shores of that island. They plundered the vessels and altar cloth on the altar of his chapel and handled them foully in his presence. When Bernard saw the holy things vilely defiled, he was revolted and felt so upset and indignant that he left the island shortly after and never returned to it. He moved back into the woods and lived there. In fact, the pirates' plundering was the Lord's will, to get Bernard off that isolated island and onto the mainland, where he could work for the good of many

3. See §140–41 for a description of life on the island. Apparently the house and chapel were built before Bernard's trip to Rome.

others and not for himself alone. When the monks of Saint-Cyprien saw that they would not have him any more, with his counsel and good will they established another as their abbot. When a few days had passed, those seafaring plunderers, who dishonored the man of God and the things on his altar on the orders of their leader, named Heobold, the cruelest of all the pirates, were submerged in ocean waves while pursuing ships that they wanted to ravage. No wonder the wretches died by drowning, when they had inflicted the same kind of death on countless numbers of the faithful. At the very hour of their deaths, an army of countless demons, in the form of a flock of ravens, gathered and filled the air with fourfold gloom. Trumpeting with a horrible sound, in fleshly forms, they struck terror into the hearts of the nearby sailors. Since the pirates had no priests, the demons gathered to celebrate their funerals. The demons took their utterly wretched souls, not so they could transport them to the joys of Paradise, but so that they could drag them to the pit of Hell with fiery scourges. A man has commenders of souls of this kind upon his departure from this life when he does not deserve to have the ministers of the Church of Christ.

61. In those days Bernard had not yet united any community and had not yet begun to establish any monastery. Since he wanted to follow the hermit life, he was secluded with a few disciples in a place called Chennedet.[4] When it was learned, from Rumor, that he would not go back to Saint-Cyprien again or come back to his dwelling on the island, an abode everyone disliked because it was difficult to reach and to leave, many people began to flock to him. They wanted to be instructed by his erudition and to be strengthened by the example of his life. Since they did not have

4. Beck, *Saint-Bernard,* 29, n. 34, and 257–58, identifies *Quercus-Docta* as Chennedet, Brittany, in the commune of Landéan, Ille-et-Vilaine, 7.9 kilometers (4.7 miles) north of Fougères. Beck describes the site as an ancient Druidic sanctuary, with megaliths, a remarkable oak tree, and a chapel named the Hermitage, whose origins are associated with Vital of Savigny, William Firmat of Fontaine-Géhard, and Bernard of Tiron.

anything to live on except what they earned by the work of their hands, sheer necessity forced them to press on with their work, and the many long psalms in honor of patrons that they recited at that time prevented them from pursuing their work for the greater part of the day. The brothers went to the holy man and asked him to make a decision about the matter. He replied, "I am afraid to omit the psalms that by custom are chanted in every monastery (*RB* 9) unless the Lord reveals otherwise, yet you must work hard from necessity. It seems fitting for us to pray earnestly meanwhile so that God may let us know somehow what we should do about this matter."

62. After eight days filled with prayer, the next night they all were overwhelmed by sleep, including Bernard, man of God, who always used to arise before the others in the depths of the night. No one could arouse himself from sleep until bright daylight flooded their eyes. Nevertheless, when they arose, they began the office, according to the *Rule,* which they required approximately half the day to complete. Through the depth of their sleep a divine revelation was sent to show them that the psalms should be omitted, particularly because, since it was winter, they customarily slept for scarcely half the night (*RB* 8:1–3). From that time Dom Bernard allowed the recitation of those psalms to be omitted and ordered his disciples to refrain from saying them thereafter. He said that he knew for certain that God preferred to have the workers earn their living than press on with such a large number of psalms. Subsequently, a nobleman named Ralph of Fougères,[5] who owned the forest where they lived, became afraid that the forest would be eradicated by their farming and could not bear it. The forest was near his castle of Fougères, and, since he greatly loved the forest, he had enclosed it by a palisade in

5. Ralph I, count of Fougères (d. 1124), son of Méen of Fougères (1030–1074), was a vassal of Count William of Mortain, the nephew of William the Conqueror. Ralph followed William the Conqueror to England and received a great deal of property from him. Ralph founded the abbey of Savigny in 1112. See *Dictionnaire d'Histoire et de Géographie Ecclesiastiques* (Paris: Letouzey et Ané, 1971), 17:1266–67.

order to keep in the wild game for his hunting. For that reason he gave them another forest named Savigny, a much better place with lands with fertile soil and abundant streams, but more than six miles away from his castle. There they constructed suitable dwellings and, although they left a few brothers in the previous place, they lived there for some years earning their living by the work of their hands. Dom Vital, whom we mentioned, had built his cell in that same forest, about two furlongs distance from them, where he later built a monastery.[6] Since Divine Providence did not want two lights so brilliant to live together, it had one of them remain there and sent the other wandering in other regions.

6. The date of this foundation is 1105. Two *stades,* less than 400 meters, or a quarter of a mile.

CHAPTER 8

Monastery Constructed in the County of Perche, Favors Accepted and Collected for Division among Others

63. A nod from Divine Providence inspired its servant Bernard and all his disciples to migrate to other regions and to leave for distant lonely places. Accordingly he sent a small group of his disciples to seek some vast desert where they could build a foundation large enough to hold them all at the same time, so none would be forced to live apart from him, which was exceedingly hard for them to bear. They derived so much consolation from his words and presence that they preferred to bear the burden of direst poverty with him than to abound in riches without him. When they found no suitable place and were returning to Bernard with no fruit from their labor; it was made known to them:

By Heaven, retrace steps in haste, and seek a fit place
For Bernard, to place him sometime in Heaven.

One of the disciples had a vision in his sleep. He saw an angelic attendant, who appeared to him as young, splendid in appearance, and becomingly dressed in a snowy garment. The angelic being placed his hand on the disciple's head and uttered these words: "Wake up quickly, arise, and make your way to Rotrou, count of Perche,[1] and you will be given what you seek." The disciple awakened immediately and related to his companions what he had seen. Making light of the vision, they returned to the teacher and reported that so far they had found no suitable dwelling for him. When after much searching two of his disciples had not found any suitable place to live, and the companion recalled his memories of the vision, they finally went to Count Rotrou and told him what they sought. The count very kindly agreed to their petition and promised that they would be given what they asked.

64. That venerable leader owned a property called Arcisses, located one mile from his castle at Nogent,[2] with fertile soil, surrounded by forests on all sides, watered by streams and springs, noted for its pleasant meadows, fit for cultivating vines and constructing buildings, and suitable for every need. There his ancestors had built a chapel, dug a fishpond, and planted orchards.

1. Kathleen Thompson (*Power and Border Lordship in Medieval France: the Counts of the Perche 1000–1226,* Royal Historical Society Studies in History, new series [Woodbridge, England: The Royal Historical Society; Rochester, N.Y.: Boydell Press, 2002], 50–85), describes the gallant career of Rotrou II, count of Perche and seigneur of Mortagne (ca. 1080–1144). During the First Crusade, he fought at the siege of Nicaea in mid-1097, commanded a division that broke out of Antioch in late June 1098, and in the final assault was the fifth man on the ladder below Bohemond and Tancred. He succeeded his father, Geoffrey II, around 1100. When he returned from Jerusalem, he married Mathilda, an illegitimate daughter of Henry I, in 1104. On behalf of his first cousin Alphonso I, king of Navarre and Aragon (1104–1134), Rotrou crusaded against the Muslims in Spain, probably in 1108. In the shipwreck of the White Ship on November 25, 1120, Rotrou's wife, Matilda, was drowned together with his two nephews, the sons of his sister Juliana and her husband, Gilbert of L'Aigle. Rotrou was governor of Tudela in Aragon and participated in campaigns from 1123 until the mid-1130s. His sister Juliana acted for him in his absence. Rotrou married Hawise, daughter of Walter of Salisbury, and returned to Perche by 1135. He fought for King Stephen and then for Empress Matilda and her husband, Geoffrey, count of Anjou, in whose service he died in 1144 during the siege of Rouen.

2. The counts of Perche, vassals of the counts of Blois and Chartres, were marcher barons who had defended Blois from incursion since the second half of the tenth century. Their castle of Saint-John at Nogent-le-Rotrou, in Eure-et-Loir, was begun around 1005 and still stands. Arcisses, in Brunelles, lies 5.5 kilometers (3.3 miles) to the east.

Rotrou led the two monks there without any delay to show them the property and granted possession of it in perpetuity to Bernard, holy man of God, and his monks. Once they had accepted it, the happy disciples were duly grateful to the giver of all good things and to the leader himself. They had not the slightest doubt that the vision which their fellow had related to them was a true one, since it was confirmed so promptly and auspiciously. They went away with orders from the count to return and they brought back the teacher, as the count himself directed. The count attentively showed him due reverence. Nonetheless, the count, misled by advice from certain individuals and obeying his mother's orders, withdrew from Bernard the gift that he had made. Nonetheless he earnestly urged the servant of God to accept another property. Beatrix,[3] the count's mother, was trying daily to remove the holy man from the vicinity of Nogent, because she was afraid that some trouble would arise because of his relationship with the monks of Cluny, having gathered many of them together in that town. Since Bernard unflinchingly withstood any blows of Fortune and could not be unduly perturbed by any setbacks, he was not shaken in the least by this one and, as ever, he was serene in mind and cheerful in countenance. He did not refuse what the count now offered and sent two disciples to explore it the following day. With the same guide as before, they came to the place, which was called Tiron. After they inspected it carefully they returned that same day to the teacher and described the place they had been shown. They said, "We have seen a place with virtually nothing required for human needs." They realized that they had labored in vain, and in dismay they prepared to return next day to the place from where they came.

65. The next night, over the property that would be accepted from the count,

3. Beatrix acted as Rotrou's regent in his absence and probably anticipated having to deal by herself with any conflict between Bernard and the Cluniac monks of Saint-Denis of Nogent-le-Rotrou.

A hanging lamp lit neighboring lands and swung
In clearest skies where Bernard saw it hung,

glittering splendidly with so many fiery rays that its circle of light bathed the entire province in a reddish glow. Which surely was a revelation to you,

To warn, indeed, order you not to refuse the count's gifts.

In the morning, while the disciples were making ready to return to their own community, Bernard himself went to see the place that they wanted to abandon. Once he reached the wood, which was called Tiron, he took care to inspect it thoroughly on foot. He was so well pleased with the appearance of the site and its location that he could not get it out of his mind. It did not linger in his mind because the region was pleasant, or its possessions were extensive, or its meadows and rivers were delightfully beautiful, or its vines were abundant, or its fertile, fruitful soil was productive, but because of the requirement imposed by the guiding revelation of Divine Providence. Once he had accepted this small property from the count, Bernard, man of the Lord, returned to his disciples, who were staying within the borders of Normandy and Brittany, so that he could gather them to himself, and lead them swiftly with him in a body to the place that he had accepted.

66. At this time, when Bernard was on the road from Nogent to Mortagne, a knight named Payen of Le Theil, traveling the same road, overtook Bernard, who was riding on a little donkey, and two of his disciples, who were walking alongside him.[4] When the knight saw them covered in their hermit rags, because of their very habit of humility and poverty, he considered them to be men of good conscience and contemptuous of the world. Since at the same time he took pity on their fatigue, he asked

4. Mortagne-au-Perche, in Orne and in the diocese of Sées, the fortified capital of Perche, is located 30.2 kilometers (18.1 miles) northwest of Nogent-le-Rotrou. Le Theil is located 11.5 kilometers (6.9 miles) southwest of Nogent-le-Rotrou.

them where they were headed. Bernard, man of God, replied that they were going to Mortagne that day, if they could. When the knight heard this, he said that he lived in that town, and with pious supplication he asked them to deign to lodge with him. The man of the Lord by no means refused the lodging offered to him from love; instead he accepted it with fitting gratitude. Along the way he tried to feed his host the bread of the word of God and to let him drink in saving religious instruction. When Payen reached Mortagne, he led the man of God to his home. He was eager to perform the all the obligations of hospitality most briskly and solicitously, so that in turn he could nourish the one from whom he had received the nourishment of heavenly wisdom on the road.

67. The enemy of humankind and the rival of all goodness, who begrudged the love of one and the nourishment of the other, and who was eager to disturb the happiness of the recipients and the extender of hospitality, so infected Payen's squire with the venom of his malice that at nightfall the squire turned to theft and stole his master's war horse.[5] When Payen learned, he was downcast, for he deeply loved the horse and knew that his physical safety depended upon the steed, for at that time there was considerable warring between the inhabitants of Bellême and Mortagne.[6] So as not to cloud the happiness of his pleas-

5. Unlike the draft horse or sumpter, which carried burdens, the war horse or charger was a large and valuable animal capable of supporting an armed knight in combat.

6. This incident probably happened ca. 1109. Rotrou II had a claim to lands in Bellême through his grandmother Adeliza, but, Robert of Bellême, his second cousin once removed, enjoyed possession of the lands through his mother, Mabel, until his downfall in 1112. In a boundary dispute before 1110, Rotrou had put Robert to flight and taken many prisoners. Orderic Vitalis (*Historia ecclesiastica,* 5: Book XIII [1–3], 395–99) describes how the crusaders returned after 1100 and repossessed their lands. Rotrou fought briefly in Spain in 1108, and upon his return a serious quarrel broke out between him and his cousin Robert, with great plundering, looting, and burning in both territories, which brought distress to their dependents, knights and peasants alike. See Marjorie Chibnall, *The World of Orderic Vitalis* (Oxford: Clarendon Press; New York: Oxford University Press, 1984), 24–25. Bellême is 16.4 kilometers (9.8 miles) south of Mortagne-au-Perche and 20.1 kilometers (12.6 miles) northwest of Nogent-le-Rotrou.

ant hospitality by the shadows of his sorrow, he put on a cheerful face, concealing his sadness, and briskly invited his guests to dine. Nonetheless, the blow to his host could not be hidden from the man of God, who tried to gladden Payen's heart with consoling words and to demonstrate to him by reason[7] that he should not grieve much over a passing matter. Yet the heavenly grace of Divine Love, by whose merits Payen had extended hospitality to his guest, wished to manifest itself.

While the thief leads the horse, grown so dumb in due
course,
He turns and, mistaken, returns what he's taken.

Divine Love allowed the thief's wit and senses to be blinded, so that he did not recognize the places, roads, and villages where he had been raised from infancy. Instead in his mind he thought Mortagne was Bellême and conversely mistook Bellême for Mortagne. Consequently, all that night he avoided Bellême, which he mistook for the enemy territory of Mortagne, and fled to the town of Mortagne as if to the safe hiding place of Bellême.

68. So, deceived by his blindness, the squire returned to Mortagne, and when he stood before the house of Payen, the host, he believed himself to be in the place where he intended to flee with the horse. When he was seized and questioned about the reason why he had returned, he came out with the truth and replied that Divine Power had coerced him to make him return that night.

As Bernard's prayers implored, what was lost is restored.

O Christ, these are your mighty works! O Christ, these are your virtues! You offered this beautiful spectacle to the world because of your friend's merit and because the thief's malice made him so drunken and dazed that he led the stolen horse back to the same persons from whom he had stolen it, as if they would shelter a

7. Bernard uses reason to cope with strong emotion on this and other occasions. See §106.

thief. So he hurried toward the ones whom his crime urged him to avoid because he was in danger of death as if he were hurrying toward loyal defenders of his life. When Payen gave thought to this incident, he tried to show his love and admiration for the man of God from that time on, not as much as he wished, but as much as he could, and later he gave a great deal of money to the monastery.

69. When Bernard completed the journey he had begun, he collected his disciples, led them with him to Tiron, and lived there with them henceforth. Therefore in the year of the Incarnation of the Word 1109, when the disciples had flocked together and received the blessing of Lord Ivo of good memory, bishop of the cathedral of Chartres,[8] he celebrated the first Mass on the holy day of Easter in the wooden monastery that was now built, which the renowned leader Rotrou had given to him with possession of property. In that true wilderness, which pleased him greatly because Heaven had foreshown it, the man of God continuously behaved in a manly and steadfast manner. He urged the brothers to build the place carefully, and informed them even more carefully of the teachings and lore of heavenly life. He said, "Now, dearest brothers, look at this desert, a very suitable place for us, quite open, conducive to silence and quiet, and appropriate for divine meditation and prayer. Here the heavy cross of Christ will be borne, here the crown of unending life will be earned, which in your piety you have long desired, and which will be conferred upon you, as you deserve, by the generosity of heavenly grace. If you are displeased that it is unsuitable for human needs, you should be pleased that a wilderness is an opportunity fit only for

8. Ivo of Chartres (ca. 1040–1115) was born in Beauvais, studied at Paris and Bec, and was elected bishop of Chartres in 1090. He was the author of the books entitled *Decretum* and *Panormia* on canon law and 288 letters on a variety of issues. He died on December 23, 1115, and was canonized at an unknown date. See John Fronton, *Vita, Ivo, Episcopus Cartonensis in Gallia,* AASS May 5: 0248E–0253D. Other comprehensive biographies of Ivo of Chartres are contained in *Gallia Christiana* 8:1126–34; and Jean Leclercq, *Correspondance/Yves de Chartres*, Les Classiques de l'Histoire de France au Moyen Age (Paris: Belles Lettres, 1949), 1:vii–xvii.

religious men and seekers of the solitary life. The harshness of this place will confer the cross and crown upon you, because, due to the lack of resources, for a long time you will not have the feigned companionship of false brothers, who may corrupt good morals by their depraved speech and bad examples."

70. At that time, because floods of rain had fallen in earlier years and the soil was too unproductive to bear crops, there was such famine[9] that many thousands died for lack of bread. The multitude of monks with Bernard had absolutely no portions of food and no money with which to buy any. Nonetheless, according to the Gospel, they concentrated on seeking the kingdom of God (Lk 12:31) and did not fear being denied the rest. To those who did not despair of divine generosity and were diligent in work and prayer, the One who kindly sent his servant Daniel a dinner through Habakkuk of Judea in Babylon (Bel and Dragon 33–40), so moved the soul of William [II], count of Nevers at that time,[10] to send a heavy gold vase from Burgundy to Bernard, man

9. Orderic Vitalis describes a feverish sickness that attacked the inhabitants of Chartres and Orléans in 1109, in combination with excessive rainfall that drowned the crops and ruined the grape harvest. For three consecutive years, 1109–1111, there was terrible famine in France (Orderic Vitalis, *Historia ecclesiastica,* 6: Book XI, 38, 40, 166–67 and 172–73).

10. William II, count of Auxerre, count of Nevers, and William III of Tonnerre, (1089–1147), succeeded his father, Renaud II, in 1095. He traveled to the Holy Land with his brother Robert and an army of 15,000 men in 1101. William II was an ally of Louis VI and spent four years as a prisoner of Thibaut IV, count of Blois and Chartres, 1116–1119, during Thibaut's war with the king of France. William II continued to fight alongside Louis VI during the wars in the 1120s and was taken prisoner a second time by Thibaut, now count of Blois and Champagne, ca. 1130–1136. He was a generous benefactor of several monasteries. Pope Eugenius III addressed him as count of Nevers in April 1146 in a letter requesting him to cease harassing the abbey of Vézelay on account of a dispute over its rights to a free election of its abbots and issues involving jurisdiction (R. B. C. Huygens, ed., *Monumenta Vizeliacensia,* in Corpus Christianorum Continuatio Medievale [Turnhout, 1976] 42:314–15, *Cartulaire,* no. 28). He declined the co-regency of France with Abbé Suger at the general parlement at Etampes on February 16, 1147, because of ill health; he entered La Grande Chartreuse shortly thereafter, and died on August 20, 1148 (*Dictionnaire de Biographie Française* [Paris: Letouzey et Ané, 1989], 17:150–51, and René de Lespinasse, *Le Nivernais et les comtes de Nevers* [Paris, 1909], 1:309). The reference to William II's being count of Nevers at that time indicates that Geoffrey was writing

of God, secluded in the most solitary wildernesses of the forests of Perche, whom he knew only by Rumor at that time. By selling the vase Bernard was able to buy enough portions of food for the monks living with him at that time and the beggars as well. Encouraged by the sign from God, and comforted by frequent sermons from the man of God, the monks girded themselves to build the premises. They applied themselves to the work but did not neglect their religious observance of prayer and silence.

71. They were fervent in holiness and ready to bear any burden of poverty, but the people living in that region had never seen their like. They wore some sort of monk's habit, but one that was cheap, coarse, rough, quite unlike the habits of other monks and quite like the very sheep[11] from which the habit was taken. Their poverty forced them to have apparel that was at a reasonable cost (*RB* 55:7), and they were not deviating in the least from the *Rule of Saint Benedict,* which they professed.[12] But the boorish brutes living in those parts were put off by habits of this unfamiliar kind and thought the men were not monks but Saracens[13] who had come through underground caves to spy on them. Troubled by Rumor, the natives in the neighborhood sent out scouts. When they drew near, the scouts observed unwarlike unarmed men who were not building evil contraptions but modest cells, who were not raising castles or towers, and who were not shrieking war cries but reciting psalms and singing hymns.

---

after the count abdicated in mid-1147. Nevers, the capital of the Nivernais region, in Nièvre, was part of the kingdom or duchy of Burgundy and located at the confluence of the Loire and the Allier.

11. Merlet, *Cartulaire de Tiron,* 1:x, cites Jacques de Vitry, *Histoire d'Occident.* Like members of other eremitical orders, the Tironian monks adopted a different habit from the regular Benedictines. At first they were shaggily attired in coarse wool and sheepskin, but later they adopted a gray habit and were known as the gray monks. Undyed wool from black sheep is a dark gray color. Years later they wore the Benedictine black.

12. See §58 for profession of the *Rule of Saint Benedict. RB* 55:7 requires the monks to use what clothing is available in the vicinity at a reasonable cost.

13. Saracens are presented as worshippers of Lucifer in Jerome, *Vita S. Hilarionis,* 3, 16, 0051F.

72. The scouts returned with better reports, beating their criminal breasts, and announced that the monks were not Saracens but new prophets sent by God to dwell in the desert. When this news was reported, rich and poor alike hurried there eager to see them. When the holy man saw this multitude arrive, he appeared in public and addressed the people. He taught them whom they should fear and serve, come whatever may. He exhorted them to prefer Heaven to earthly things and to exchange the transitory for the eternal. He taught those who flocked to him. He declared how glorious and wonderful man is when he becomes godlike by sharing in the Supreme Good. He demonstrated that happiness in this life is scarce and fleeting and confirmed the dreadful and eternal torments that await sinners in Hell after death. Many terrified and remorseful persons renounced the world and, by taking the monastic habit, submitted themselves to his instructions (*RB* Prol.:50).

73. While our page shows scant esteem for a few things, it does not omit those things by which Highest Providence earnestly desired to show the holiness of its soldier. When the man of the Lord had just come to live in the wilderness of Tiron, his cowherd once was negligent and left a calf in the woods. When the cowherd realized the calf was missing, he searched for it carefully throughout the wood but did not find it. Two days later the man of the Lord, who was sitting outside in the shade of a tree with a few brothers by his cell door, saw a wolf slowly emerge with the calf from the dark woods. So the calf would not stray from the path running from the woods to the man of God's cell through the level ground of some fields, the wolf drove it slowly, threatening to swat it with his tail. O wonder!

> The biting wolf becomes the calf's guardian and restorer
> And restrains his greedy starving teeth.

As the wolf came straight toward them, the monks who were with the servant of God recognized the calf as one of their own, the one their cowherd had lost. Thunderstruck and stupefied, they marveled that despite his greedy gluttony the raging wolf had not only refrained from seizing the calf but had also herded it and brought it back, which was beyond belief. The wolf, not terrified in the least by the presence of the monks, was not afraid to draw near to the feet of the man of God. The wolf paused for a bit, looking at him with a pleasant expression, and, bowing his head as if committing his calf to Bernard, returned to the woods. O mighty innocence of the most holy Bernard! O his overwhelming humility! which constrains the beast's ferociousness, so that it does not try to do harm but is forced to be good.

74. Bernard, man of God, who overflowed with feelings of Divine Love and trusted in the generosity of the kindness of God, strengthened by the example of the one who said: him who comes to me I will not cast out (Jn 6:37), did not want to turn anyone away. Instead he tried by word and example to restore all to be conformed to Christ (Rom 8:29). Many monks, holy and religious men, from various monasteries, inspired by Rumor's description of his holiness, hurriedly flocked to him in order to see a new Antony living in the desert and to follow in his footsteps of poverty. Many noblemen from all parts arrived, longing to enlist as raw recruits of Almighty God and to live with Bernard. Some of them would offer their sons and kinsmen to the Lord to be educated under Bernard's instructions, many of whom achieved the summit of perfection through the precepts and example of the servant of God and later, when they were chosen to rule religious foundations, became abbots of various monasteries.

75. One day, when Bernard, man of God, was blessing the monks, one of them, named Liger, a religious man and a priest, saw roses fall from the heights of the air,

On those monks he enfolds and by his way of life molds.

By the sign of this external miracle, the Lord wanted to show either His confessor's merit or his ability to restore human consciences to the flowery life of holiness. After a single year had run its course, a certain monk who was present, whose name was Antiquillus, a man of great integrity and innocence, saw that:

> While Bernard, senior, in doing good not tardy
> is offering to on high and proffering chants,
> Snow and dew alike fall down on them, clear to all
> from on high descend blooms as well as perfumes.

By such a wondrous display, the Divine Will was pleased to show the privileged status of its soldier or the purity and celibacy of monastic life.

76. One spring day, while Bernard, man of the Lord, was deep in contemplation in the oratory and the brothers were working far away, a fire invaded the dry forest. The fire was swept along by violent blasts of wind until it reached the thickest part of the thorn bushes that surrounded their cells on all sides. The thorn bushes burst into flames, and the fire was at the point of consuming all their workrooms. The brothers fought long and hard to extinguish the sweeping fire and were completely unsuccessful. In despair, they entered their cells and carried all their household goods onto the cleared and level fields. They tearfully abandoned their entire foundation, which they thought would soon be burned up by the fire. Hearing their commotion, the servant of the Lord came out of the oratory, and

> When he saw the great wind and fire, compassionate,

with holy water he aspersed the flames, which were just starting to invade the workrooms, so that:

> He restrained the flames' fervor and the wind's furor
> So they could not proceed, and by prayers made them
> recede.

The fire did not presume to cross the boundaries of his aspersion. Instead, it turned against the wind's force and on itself, subsided and went out. O what great merit this man possesses, when his will can even restrain the elements!

CHAPTER 9

Monastery Built on the Thironne River. Favors Granted by Count Rotrou

77. At that time, so that Bernard, soldier of Christ, would not lack toil and tribulation to combat, the monks of Saint-Denis said that they were entitled to the tithes and burial fees[1] of the very tract that Count Rotrou had given to him. This malicious claim forced him to abandon the buildings that his disciples had constructed so laboriously and to seek another site where he might be allowed to dwell. Therefore he went to the above-mentioned Ivo, the venerable bishop of the celebrated cathedral of Chartres, dedicated in honor of Holy and Ever-Virgin Mary,[2] and to the canons at that time, and he asked them to give

1. Monasteries both paid and were owed tithes. Local inhabitants paid tithes on their domestic production to the overlord or to a monastery. If they owed tithes to Tiron, the monastery's income was reduced when the tithes were paid to Saint-Denis. In addition, persons who cleared and cultivated wasteland eventually owed noval tithes on the new land under production. See Giles Constable, *Monastic Tithes, from their Origins to the Twelfth Century,* Cambridge Studies in Medieval Life and Thought, new series, 10 (Cambridge: Cambridge University Press, 1964), 105–6. In 1129, Saint-Denis turned over the tithe on Old Tiron to Tiron Abbey (Merlet, *Cartulaire de Tiron,* 1:139–40, no. 118). Some of these tithes seem to be noval tithes on fields, vineyards, and a garden or wheat field cleared and planted by Bernard's disciples at Tiron-Brunelles. If Saint-Denis imposed both noval tithes and burial fees during an epidemic and famine, the financial strain might well have forced Bernard to move his foundation out of the parish of Brunelles into the adjacent parish of Gardais.

2. Chartres has been a pilgrimage center for the veneration of Mary since the seventh century.

him a very small portion of a farm that they owned, contiguous to his little property, on which he might found his monastery. The canons owned a hamlet named Gardais adjacent to the little tract that the count had given to the man of God. The canons received the servant of God with due veneration, listened to him with kindness and good will, and, in their noble magnificence and generous munificence, granted him more land than he had requested. Once the donation was made, they drew up the charter[3] and sent Lord Geoffrey, a cathedral canon and the provost of that property, with some other persons, to inspect the tract.[4] After they came to the aforesaid farm alongside the stream called the Thironne, as the cathedral chapter had decreed, they gave him the tract he had requested to build the workrooms of his monastery, in freehold[5] as they themselves had held it.

78. At that time, a matron born of royal lineage named Adela, countess of Blois,[6] made several offers to the holy Bernard of broader expanses of land on which to build his monastery and

3. A charter dated February 3, 1114, confirms that the chapter at Chartres granted Bernard a carucate of land in the parish of Gardais (Merlet, *Cartulaire de Tiron,* 1:1–2, no. 1). In 1114 Rotrou gave Tiron-Gardais a cemetery, which was consecrated by Ivo of Chartres with a statement that the monastery was under his protection (ibid., 13–14, no. 2). A duplicate is in the letters of Ivo, bishop of Chartres (PL 162:0283A–D, no. 283).

4. Beck (*Saint-Bernard,* 400, n. e) notes that Canon Geoffrey II of Lèves held the provostship of Fontenay-sur-Eure, of which the parish of Gardais was a dependency. The property was contiguous to the first foundation at the swamp that was the source of the Thironne River but extended to the east toward the hamlet of Gardais and lay outside the boundary of the parish of Brunelles.

5. Tiron Abbey had title to the land for an indeterminate duration and held it in free tenure, owing the overlord certain free services.

6. Adela, the third daughter of William the Conqueror, duke of Normandy, born after her father became king of England and hence of royal blood, was married to Stephen-Henry, count of Blois and Chartres, in 1084. Pious, literary, and an excellent administrator, upon her husband's death in 1102 during the First Crusade she acted as regent during the minority of his successor, her second son, Thibaut. In 1122 Adela entered the convent of Marcigny, where she died in 1137. *Dictionnaire de Biographie Française* (Paris: Librairie Letouzey et Ané, 1932), 1:529. See Kimberly A. LoPrete, "Adela of Blois: Familial Alliances and Female Lordship," in *Aristocratic Women in Medieval France,* ed. Theodore Evergates (Philadelphia: University of Pennsylvania Press, 1999), 7–43.

much more suitable sites. Nonetheless he refused, because he preferred to place his monastic foundation under the protection of Blessed Ever-Virgin Mary than under the advocacy[7] of any layperson whomsoever. The canons were extremely pleased they had consented to have such a tenant on one of their cathedral farms. In their compassion, they loved him deeply throughout his entire lifetime, gave him many good things as well as liturgical ornaments, carefully extended their patronage, devotedly and vigilantly protected the possessions of the monastery itself, and skillfully shielded it from certain troublemakers. After Bernard had established his foundation as a possession of the Blessed Mother of God, he venerated her so lovingly thereafter that he instituted a special daily Mass to be celebrated perpetually in her honor, for the salvation of all the benefactors of his monastery, and, above all, the canons, which is solemnly celebrated to this day.[8]

79. Meanwhile, Count Rotrou, whom Bernard, holy man of the Lord, cherished more than any other mortal man, was captured violently by Fulk, count of Anjou and subsequently king of Jerusalem.[9] Fulk held Rotrou in chains in his power, not because he was arranging to release him, but so he could extort the maximum amount of money for him from Robert of Bellême, a viciously cruel monster.[10] Robert paid the enormous price to

7. An advocate was the lay protector and legal representative of a monastery. An advowry was a well-remunerated office often held and indeed claimed by a local magnate, who could thus influence monastic affairs.

8. The daily Mass Bernard instituted, known as *la Mère-Dieu,* was said until the abbey of Tiron was destroyed almost seven centuries later (Merlet, *Cartulaire de Tiron,* 1:xiii).

9. Fulk V, count of Anjou, whose daughter Mathilda married William Adelin, son of Henry I, in 1119, made a donation to the priory of Reuzé near Châtellerault (Merlet, *Cartulaire de Tiron,* 1: 189, no. 165; 2: 297). Fulk V became king of Jerusalem in 1131.

10. C. Warren Hollister notes that Robert of Bellême was an intelligent, powerful, and vicious Norman magnate with thirty-four castles whom Henry I endeavored to retain as an ally, in *Henry I,* ed. Amanda Clark Frost, Yale English Monarchs (New Haven, Conn.: Yale University Press, 2001), 154–55.

purchase Count Rotrou from Fulk, not because Robert wanted any ransom from the count, but because he wanted to torture him to death by various ways in his prisons. Robert felt such tremendous hatred for Rotrou, because in open warfare he had been defeated by Rotrou with his army and put to flight,[11] that he preferred a miserable death for Rotrou to a prosperous life for himself. By order of this tyrant, devices and preparations were made. The feet of the noble leader were bound to the torture post; his shins were enclosed in many rings and fetters; his hands and arms were covered with mail gloves; and an enormous weight of numerous irons and different types of chains was hung around his neck. Contorted and racked by so tight and crushing a covering, fashioned with industry and skill, Rotrou was thrown back into a narrow dungeon, and, so he might not die too quickly, Robert added that he was to be fed something or other twice a week.

80. After Count Rotrou learned of his fate, through the legate[12] he ordered his mother and his vassal lords to consider him dead and to establish another overlord. He asked his mother to inform Bernard, man of God, so that Bernard could intercede for the salvation of his soul and have no concern about rescuing his body, which was utterly impossible. When the man of God heard this message, his eyes flooded with tears. Then, filled with prophetic spirit, he admonished the messengers to trust in God's mercy and not to despair in the least of Rotrou's release. He added that this misfortune would be turned into good fortune for Rotrou and into direst misfortune for Robert. So it occurred. By a single foresighted plan of the one who knew how to take the wise in their own craftiness (Jb 5:13), within a few days, as the man of God predicted, the count was free and restored safe and

11. The reference is to the boundary dispute in 1109, in which Payen of Le Theil was embroiled.

12. Hildebert of Lavardin, bishop of Le Mans and papal legate, described his visit to Rotrou in prison and his own imprisonment by Rotrou's mother in *Epistolae,* Book II, PL 171: 0225B–0228B, nos. 17–18.

sound to his native land, and Robert was fettered in the aforementioned chains, by the order of King Henry [I], transported to England, and confined in perpetual imprisonment until the day of his death.[13] O man worthy of greatest public commendation! Whose tears produced a wellspring of compassion, whose exhortations encouraged a bereft land! According to Bernard's prophecy, while the captive was released, the tyrant, trapped in his own snares, was delivered up into exile.

81. The count, who was restored to his native land and earlier good fortune, soon acquired the castle of Bellême with its outlying land and also subjugated the lands that he and his ancestors had once possessed.[14] As soon as he could, he came to Bernard, man of God, by whose merits and prayers he had been freed. He fully expressed the gratitude he owed Bernard, not only in words but also in tears and by subsequent signs. For he so cherished Bernard thereafter that he obeyed Bernard in many things, curtailed the pillaging and cruelty he had learned, reformed and led a better life. So he would not seem ungrateful for such a favor, he gave Bernard many gifts, which we will refrain from listing lest our devoted readers find us tedious. Were we to itemize the many kinds of ornaments for the church, gems, gold or silver vases, pleasant lands, farms, and woods, control of ponds, vineyards, and mills, and income from various tithes that he gave to

13. Thompson (*Power and Border Lordship,* 61) notes: "A number of Norman magnates who had never been reconciled to Henry's rule, including . . . Robert of Bellême, rose in rebellion against the king." By siding with Fulk of Anjou against Henry I, Robert was guilty of treason. The downfall, trial, and life imprisonment of Robert of Bellême are described by William of Malmesbury, *Gesta regum Anglorum,* Book V, 398, 626; and Orderic Vitalis, *Historia ecclesiastica,* 6: Book XI, 44, 178–79. Chibnall states that Robert was summoned to appear before Henry I on November 4, 1112, was tried, was imprisoned in fetters, and was still alive in 1130–1131 (178, n. 1, and 179, n. 3).

14. Rotrou and Thibaut, count of Blois and Chartres, captured the castle of Bellême on May 1, 1113 (Orderic Vitalis, *Historia ecclesiastica,* 6: Book XI, 45, 183). Henry I awarded the castle and estate to Rotrou. The imprisonment of Robert of Bellême and Rotrou's succession as count of Bellême are described by William of Jumièges, *Gesta Normannorum Ducum, Orderic Vitalis, and Robert of Torigni,* ed. Elisabeth M. C. Van Houts (Oxford: Clarendon Press, 1995), 2: Book VIII, 35, 264–65.

our monastery, we would seem to be fabricating a tale and not describing the deeds of the holy man. Rotrou returned the property [Arcisses] we mentioned earlier, which, misled by the advice he had received, he had taken from the blessed man. He made room for many of Bernard's monks there, after suitable dwellings were built and many sources of income were allocated. The above-mentioned Beatrix, who recognized Bernard's holiness, ceased to reside in her castle, once houses were built at Tiron. She lived at Tiron for the rest of her life and built the large basilica church with many cash outlays. When Beatrix died, her daughter Juliana,[15] who had inherited her mother's goodness, succeeded her, and subsequently she carefully completed a considerable part of our workrooms by many separate outlays.[16]

82. While Bernard was building his monastery in Frankland, Robert of Arbrissel had constructed his monastery in Aquitaine at Fontevraud, Ralph of la Futaye[17] had constructed his in Brittany, and Vital of Mortain was building his monastery in Normandy, at Savigny in the diocese of Avranches, which he subsequently turned over to Dom Bernard, with its dependent monasteries.[18] The Heavenly Judge wanted them to remain far from Bernard and separated in various regions, because each one built so many monasteries that it was impossible for a single region to hold them all and a single province to contain all the communities they founded. When Bernard, soldier of Christ,

15. This passage indicates that Beatrix and Juliana acted for Rotrou while living at a house at Tiron instead of the family castle at Nogent-le-Rotrou. Thus Tiron was an administrative center of Perche and had noblewomen in residence who were not nuns. Thompson (*Power and Border Lordship,* 74) mentions Juliana's regency during Rotrou's absence.

16. Orderic Vitalis (*Historia ecclesiastica,* 4: Book VIII, 27, 330–31) confirms Beatrix's contributions.

17. Beck (*Saint-Bernard,* 48) notes different spellings of the names of Robert of Arbrissel as *Robertus de Abrisello,* §20, *Robertus de Abresello,* §49, and *Robertus Abreselensis* here. Ralph of la Futaie is spelled *Radulphus de Fusteia,* §20 and *Radulphus Fusteiensis* here. The variation suggests different narrators.

18. Savigny's merger with Cîteaux occurred in 1147 under St. Bernard, abbot of Clairvaux.

had established his monastic foundation on the farm that the Mother of God had given to him through her canons, no malicious claims could expel him, no adversities caused by violent storms could move him, because he clung to Christ, the firm solidity of immovable stability.

CHAPTER 10

Revelation of Subsequent Eternal Salvation of Two Monks. Some Miracles

83. One night, while the brothers were chanting the psalms appointed for nocturns (*RB,* 9–11)[1] in the oratory, a brother reached the point of death. Accordingly, when the clappers were struck according to the ritual, the brothers gathered together. They wanted to conduct the funeral service of the now-dead brother promptly and return to the oratory, so that they could complete the remainder of the interrupted psalms. Something other than they intended occurred, for a delay made it necessary for them to remain there longer. The infirmarian did not have water to wash the lifeless limbs of the dead brother and could not prepare the corpse for burial, because he could not find the key to the door leading out to the spring. Terribly upset on this account, he seized an axe in order to break down the door. Bernard, holy man of God, gently restrained his agitated movement and restored the key to him, which had been hidden by the Devil. It was the key for which he had searched so long and had been unable to find. When the funeral service had been conducted, they returned to the church and finished the required portion of the uncompleted

1. There are never fewer than twelve psalms, not counting Psalms 3 and 94. This long office, known as vigils, nocturns, or matins, is celebrated in the middle of the night.

divine office. Afterward, when the brothers were discussing the delay among themselves on the following day, Bernard, soldier of Christ, said that a brother who had [not] been present at the funeral service had seen such a multitude of demons coming to call the brother's soul to account that they filled the whole valley in which the monastery was located. Since the demons were not able to deprive him of his salvation, as they tried to do, they raised the impediment of delaying his burial. In truth we knew for certain that what he said was false, for we knew for certain that no one was absent from the brother's funeral service except the one who was disclosing what he had seen, so we had not the slightest doubt that he was speaking of himself.[2]

84. At that same time, when the monks were preparing to bury the body of a brother who had led an exceedingly worthy religious life, and they were chanting the proper amount of psalms, Bernard, man of God, went to the oratory in order to pray more privately. For a long time he commended the soul of the dead brother to God in his prayers. Heavenly Mercy heard Bernard with joy, as later became clear, and kindly wished to confirm the brother's salvation immediately, so that Bernard would have no doubt about it. The brother, whose body was on the bier, appeared in utmost splendor to Bernard, who, as we said previously, was deep in prayer. The brother was clothed in a white garment, holding a maniple[3] in his hand. After he asked for a blessing from Bernard, he entered into conversation and earnestly entreated Bernard to greet his brothers on his behalf and to tell them that now he was able to be at rest.

2. Beck (*Saint-Bernard,* 405, n. 1) notes: "Paragraph 83 poses some translation problems and may have been inaccurately retranscribed by the copyists. The expression *'exsequis interfuisse'* should normally be translated as 'who attended the funeral service.' But the end of the text stipulates that this monk was the only one absent from the Office for the Dead, if at least the verb *affuisse* used here is correctly written for *abfuisse.*" Logically Bernard and the infirmarian would have been alone with the corpse preparing it for burial while the funeral service was conducted.

3. A maniple is a Eucharistic vestment, an ornamental band worn above the left wrist.

85. A knight named Robert of La Motte[4] lived in the vicinity of our monastery. At that time, he was not yet overflowing with worldly goods, which we have known him to be subsequently. He had long been oppressed by poverty, to the astonishment of his neighbors, for he seemed to be entitled to an exceedingly high income from towns and farms. Others found the misfortune of his impoverishment particularly astonishing because it was said that he customarily managed his affairs with diligence and cautious prudence in all things. He came in good faith to the man of God, with whom he was already on good terms, and with devout prayers he urged Bernard to honor his home by coming in person and presumed to add that he hoped Bernard would stay with him for a single night. Since Bernard was exceedingly kind, he willingly consented to this pious request, came to the home, and accepted the hospitality. What more can I say?

With riches filled, but not an earthly trove,
The new guest to the knight's home came and drove
His poorness hence, so rich in all he throve.

There was such abundance in the knight's home from that time on, as became public later, that he rejoiced at having extended hospitality in his home not to the servant of God but to the very Lord of all generosity and kindness. Subsequently the knight did not forget how he had come to so much external opulence and was never ungrateful. From then on, insofar as he was able, he provided for Bernard continuously, and after Bernard's death he gave us several good things and enriched our monastery by income from a great many tithes.[5]

4. Merlet (*Cartulaire de Tiron,* 2:288) situates La Motte in Champrond-en-Perchet, 3.5 kilometers (2.1 miles) southeast of Nogent-le-Rotrou.

5. Ibid., 1:100–101, no. 81. These donations, confirmed by the cartulary, were clearly made after Bernard's death. Robert's tithes were included in the gift of the church of Argenvilliers by Geoffrey II, bishop of Chartres, ca. 1126. Robert gave the monastery the church of Saint-Lubin-des-Cinq-Fonds and the tithes of the parish of Argenvilliers ca. 1132 (ibid., 188, no. 164), and he appears as a witness in other charters.

86. At Saint-Lubin-des-Cinq-Fonds[6] there was a little boy who had had a fleshy tumor growing over and covering his entire eye from the day he was born. When his mother heard that Bernard, man of the Lord, would be passing through that town, as soon as she could, she presented her offspring for his inspection and tearfully tried to make him place his hand on her only son. Because the holy man was moved by the mother's sobbing and agreed to satisfy the people standing around,

When he saw morbid growth and how the orb did,
His prayers and worthy cross's sign sufficed
To heal the blinded child in praise of Christ.

Bernard restored him swiftly to health, and all the morbid growth vanished at the sign of the cross.

87. Such a multitude of men flocked to the servant of God, because they longed to renounce the world and wanted to benefit from his learning, that within three years the Father had five hundred monks.[7] O wonderful man, born not for himself alone but for all! See how he did not work for himself alone but for all who seek the truth! In this alone he was pleasing to the Holy Spirit, for, as Solomon attests, these things are beautiful in the sight of God and of mortals: agreement among brothers and sisters, friendship among neighbors (Ecclus 25:1–2). He kept three hundred of them with him; he sent two hundred out to live in priories by twelves in various parts of the world. Divine Mercy in its great generosity, which continuously feeds the birds of the

6. Saint-Lubin-des-Cinq-Fonds, north of Authon-du-Perche, is about 12 kilometers (7.2 miles) south of Nogent-le-Rotrou.

7. *William of Malmesbury's Chronicle of the Kings of England,* trans. John Sharpe, ed. J. A. Giles, Bohn's Antiquarian Library (London: Henry G. Bohn, 1847, reprinted New York: AMS Press, 1968), 471, refers to Bernard, abbot of Tiron: "The other, a noted admirer of poverty, leaving a most opulent monastery, retired with a few followers into a woody and sequestered place, and there, 'As a lamp could not be hidden under the bushel basket,' vast numbers flocking to him, he founded a monastery, more celebrated for the piety and number of the monks than for the splendour and extent of its riches." For the Latin text, see William of Malmesbury, *Gesta Regum Anglorum,* Book V, 440, 512.

air (Mt 6:26), most kindly provided continuously for those who suffered from great poverty and, because of the faith of the holy man, obtained food for them. Nonetheless, many days there was a shortage of bread, so that a pound of bread (*RB* 39:4)[8] had to be divided between two and sometimes among four. Sometimes they had no bread at all, instead they stayed alive by eating merely greens and pulses. Better keep silent than say anything about wine.[9] They did not have wine; they did not try to have wine at that time. During that exceedingly harsh winter many had no pelisses and more had no cowls. It was a time when the cold was extremely bitter and the clothing on their frail mortal bodies was scarcely enough to keep them alive. Since they were oppressed by such a shortage of things of this world, they rejoiced greatly at bearing the burden of such dire poverty for Christ. They had worldly goods aplenty in the presence of their most holy Father Bernard, who was full of divine consolation. While he lived among them, he restored their minds with heavenly words of instruction, and the disciples were filled with so much love for the Godhead that they rejoiced more greatly in such loving instruction than they would have rejoiced if they had had passing things aplenty in his absence. When they had no bread at all and ate only greens or pulses, as we said, they were so strengthened by the consolation and presence of the man of God that they regularly and eagerly did deeds that were pleasing to God and believed that they were visited and consoled by Him. Their abstinence in food and drink and clothing was greater than is required by the *Rule of Saint Benedict,* father and founder of monks, or is decreed by any other written regulations (*RB* 73:5).

88. At that same time Bernard, man of the Lord, restored to perfect health a brother named Odo, who was filled with a de-

8. *RB* 39:4 provides for a generous pound of bread per person as part of the daily portion of food.

9. *RB* 40:3 allows a half bottle of wine as a daily portion, the equivalent of 0.273 liters (.57 pint).

monic spirit, by making the sign of the cross over him and ordering him to be released from the chains in which he was bound. When Odo was released, he became calm once more and was peaceable, as if he had not suffered from any earlier insanity. We want to include another miracle now to disclose how Bernard, soldier of Christ, was enlightened by the spirit of prophecy. One day he went to Chartres on business,[10] but, before he began to conduct it, to the surprise of his companions who were with him, he returned to the monastery unexpectedly. When he asked the brothers if anything untoward had happened after his departure, they informed him that a brother named Gervais, tormented by an evil spirit, was being held fettered in an infirmary cell. At once the man of God told us who were gathered around him that he had known of it when he was in Chartres and had returned hastily for that reason. He ordered Gervais to be released from his chains and led to him. When Gervais was led in, the servant of God restored him to peacefulness by marking him with the sign of the cross, and afterward he was released from his insanity by Divine Clemency because of the merit of his confessor.

89. In summertime, when the brothers were bringing in the hay harvest and conveying it in wagons and other vehicles to lay up within the enclosure of the monastery, that very day misfortune struck, undoubtedly by permission of the One without whose nod no leaves wither on the tree (Ps 1:3), but notwithstanding which troubled their minds. A little boy, whose name was Amelin, rushed heedlessly to help with a cart (which was visibly so heavily laden with hay that it could scarcely be drawn by ten or more). Amelin fell backward and was promptly overtaken by the heavy rolling edges of the nearby wheels, which passed right over him and laid him out on his back. Since those around

10. Bernard might have had monastic business to transact with the cathedral canons or have been marketing Tiron's livestock and crafts. Chartres is a long day's journey of 39.8 kilometers (23.9 miles) from Tiron, so Bernard's premonition must have made him seriously concerned about the situation in his monastery.

him believed him to be all but dead, they decided that all they could do would be to conduct his burial. In tears they arranged his shattered limbs on a tool commonly called a winnowing fork and took him to the infirmary cell half dead and scarcely quivering. Then Bernard, who was in the oratory as was his custom, learned of it and hurried as quickly as possible, heedless of his steps, to the pallet where the wretched young beginner was lying. First, mindful of the Lord's announcement, he did not fail to greet the cell with "Peace be with you" (Jn 20:19, 26) and the sign of the blessed cross. What a miracle! The one who was thought to be all but dead was roused by Bernard's voice and opened his eyes when Bernard entered. When the servant of God placed his hand on him, he promptly recovered. So the one who was almost borne by the hands of others for burial got up on his own feet and (we were seeing this and magnifying the Lord on high) (Lk 1:46) returned to the outside community safe and sound.

90. As long as the man of God had breath in his body, none of his disciples was idle. Everyone worked with his own hands at appointed hours, unless prevented by some impediment. His disciples included numerous artisans, who practiced their individual crafts (*RB* 57) in silence. Subpriors always monitored them, so that, by the Father's order, they were diligent in strict observation of the *Rule* (*RB* 6). If one of them was compelled to speak from some unavoidable necessity, he refrained from rattling or prattling, because the *Rule* did not let idle talkers go unpunished. Although the venerable Father imposed subpriors on all individuals, as we said, nonetheless he made his own rounds inspecting everyone and, since he recalled the words of the apostle: if any one will not work, let him not eat (2 Thes 3: 10), he allowed no one to be idle. Then such humility increased in their hearts, because of the example of the man of God, that they eagerly performed any humble work with their own hands. They carried firewood on their shoulders from the forest, took turns cooking unassisted by any servants, and never engaged in any rebellion,

disobedience, and insolence. The example of the man of God made their minds aspire to such heights of love that they loved one another unfeignedly and outdid one another in respectfulness. They abandoned their own wills and submitted to the wills of others, they postponed what was convenient to themselves and did what was convenient to others, and they commiserated in all ways with their wretched brothers.

CHAPTER 11

Hospitality. Spirit of Prophecy. Rumor's Report of Holiness

91. A newly professed monk, one of the man's disciples, began to wonder about Bernard and was thunderstruck

By Rumor's proclamation of his reputation,

when he had not seen Bernard raise the dead to light, cleanse the lepers' blight, or restore the blind their sight (Mt 10:8, 11:5). The disciple was failing to consider that holiness of life does not come from performing miracles but from bringing light and doing justice. For a very long time he continued these deliberations and spied constantly on Bernard's way of life. Then, one night there came

A great lantern in sight, full of radiant light,
Borne back by none and forth by none, whose glow
Led Bernard whether he went to or fro.

It was Bernard's custom never to be preceded by a lamp, carried either by himself or by another. When we asked him why he went without a light in the night, he replied because, like us, he knew how to get to all the doors of the house. For that reason, this spy

Observed with surprise a great lamp of this wise.

As soon as he could the next day, he told the man of God what he had seen and shamelessly admitted how he had been assessing Bernard's way of life. The holy Bernard assured him that his eyes could be deceived and forbade him menacingly to be deceived anymore about this matter. It is indisputably clear that the Lord meant the lantern, which bears light for travelers, to signify the abundant light of the works of His confessor, which leads the way for all His followers.

92. Bernard, man of the Lord, extended hospitality eagerly to all comers. He excluded no one from his guest house and instructed his monks to admit everybody: the rich, the poor, the lame, the weak, little infants, girls and women, lepers, persons with every kind of illness; he excluded no one on grounds of sex or age. Instead, gathering together all kinds of persons in his guest house, he met all their needs as best he could. The poorer they were, the more generously he served them and happily made preparations to give them food and feasts, insofar as he had stores at hand. Many times, by chance, because he did not have anything else, he took from the table the bread that had been placed before the brothers in the refectory and gladly placed it before his guests. His whole community behaved this way to all comers, and on several occasions the community unshod its own horses to shoe their guests' horses. In the bitterest winter cold, many times he took off garments that were not superfluous with which he mercifully clothed nude paupers. No one who went to him in need was sent away empty-handed (Mk 12:3). He robbed his own to clothe the unknown and lent assistance to all. How many times he was willing to be obliging, or how many times he endured being almost nude, covered only by his cowl for this reason, only He knows, from whom no things are hidden. No one gave more to the poor than he who kept nothing for himself. Since there are three types of bloodless martyrdom: chastity in youth, abstinence in abundance, and generosity in poverty, he won two in Aquita-

ine[1] and, in order to obtain the triumphal palm of the third, in Frankland he was a daily martyr. Although he was afflicted by great poverty, yet he deprived himself and his disciples of what they had and gave it to the poor and to all comers. That custom, instituted at that time, is still observed today in our monastery, where all are gathered in the guest house and are supplied with the food and bedding they require, of which stores are at hand.

93. As God is my witness, no one outshone him in the virtues of love and generosity in our time; no one extended hospitality and practiced humility more zealously; no one paid less heed to his own flesh. He imposed such rigorous abstinence upon himself that he never treated his body with medicines, never was bled, and never took a bath (*RB* 36:8); moreover, after he was a professed monk he never sat by the fire to warm his limbs. When he was young and seriously ill with a high fever, he never left the community for a single day. When he was an old man and was suffering because he had fractured a rib in an accident, he refused to take any medicine for relief from such a misfortune. Moreover he did not tell anyone he was suffering from an injury of this kind until he recovered his health. He was afflicted many times by the negligence of the refectorians, who failed to put water at his table (*RB* 56) (for the very small cup he used), and for three or four days he would eat without drinking or telling anyone about his missing drinks. Indeed, he rejoiced in finding greater abstinence and affliction with which to torment himself, and, when the servers reproached themselves, he forbade them to mention it. If therefore the temperance of those who refrain from getting drunk when they could do so is held up for universal admiration, what merit should be attributed to Bernard, who abstained from water itself? Give me someone who can be abstinent at some more elegant meal and be content with barley bread, and I will give you Bernard, who many times

1. This statement contradicts Bernard's spending his youth in Ponthieu.

lived on raw roots of greens and in very small amounts. He always ate in the community and with the brothers,[2] and as he was preeminent in place among the disciples, so he was preeminent by virtue of his abstinence. He never allowed himself to be served any savory dish whatsoever that was not being served to the whole community; instead he abstained from the very dishes others enjoyed.

94. We are clearly showing that Divine Grace conferred the spirit of prophecy upon its confessor Bernard, and we will mention a few of the many things he knew by prophetic spirit. There was a monk in his monastery named Vital, a priest by rank, who stole things that belonged to the brothers, because he intended to return to the vomit (Prv 26:11) of the secular life he had abandoned. Vital suddenly fell down one night, when he was standing in choir with the chanters. The next day when the brothers asked why he had fallen so disgracefully, he replied that he had been overwhelmed by sleep, which made him collapse. But the holy Bernard contradicted him and said, "Brother, what you have said is not so. In the night I saw a demon, which caused that fall when it rose up horrifyingly before you. Unless you swiftly purge your conscience by confessing the bad deed you have committed and repent of the evil intention in which you are ensnared, that demon will make you fall lower yet."

O wondrous man, whose penetration merits veneration,
Whose mind reveals what speech conceals;
He grasps the monk's intention and his plan
And shows the crime and madness of the man.

Bernard saw the spectral forms of the demons and knew the sins of men, whose hearts' secrets are not hidden. As Bernard foretold, not much time later, we saw that was what happened. The monk abandoned monastic life, returned to his former depravity,

2. Tiron had the aforementioned abbot's table prescribed in *RB* 56, but some abbots had separate houses where they ate and slept apart from the community.

and clung for another five years to the concubine whom he had kept improperly before he professed as a monk.

95. By this time Rumor's report of the holy man, spreading further and further daily and bearing tidings on its swift wings of the signs of his virtues throughout the world, portrayed him to listeners in order to tell the measure of his stature. Rumor described the features of his open face, in which his good morals, pious innocence, and gentle soul were depicted, as he appeared on his seal.[3] Rumor portrayed the rigorousness of his abstinence and the holiness of his life, the fullness of his many years, and the whiteness of his hair. By this portrait Rumor made the absent man seem almost present in their eyes and made him known and loved by all. Not only was he acclaimed throughout the nearby parts of the region of Gaul but his praise was conveyed to the farthest ends of Burgundy, the Midi [*Alani*],[4] and Aquitaine; it spread to the Anglo-Norman and British borders and went as far as Albania of the Scots, and its impact became evident subsequently. From the outer boundaries of all these regions many persons hastened to Bernard, so they could experience the physical presence of the one whom they already knew about from Rumor, hear counsel from his lips as they taught salvation, and learn for themselves the signs of his virtues. Some of them took care to give many cash gifts to his monastery, and others, because they could not have him physically with them at the outer boundaries

3. This passage indicates that as abbot Bernard had a personal seal on which his face was carved.

4. J. Corblet (*Hagiographie du diocèse d'Amiens* [Paris: J.-B. Dumoulin, and Amiens: Prevost-Allo, 1868], 1:300–301, n. 2) summarizes the debate about the meaning of *Alanorum*, or the Alains, a people who once invaded Gaul and went on into Spain, giving their name to Catalonia. He notes that the Bollandists thought the reading should be *Alamannorum* or Germans, because the Alains left Europe in the fifth century, but that D. Clement (*Histoire littéraire de la France,* 12) notes that a colony of Alains remained in Gaul in the Midi and could have survived until the twelfth century. In fact, Germany and Midi are correct renderings, for the Tironian priory of Joug-Dieu was located at Saint-Georges-de-Reneins, 8.3 kilometers (5 miles) north of Villefranche-sur-Saone in Beaujolais, a region bordering on the Midi whose overlord was the German king Lothair.

of their regions, took back twelve of his monks and then began to build monasteries for them in their territories.[5]

96. One of these benefactors, Henry I, king of England and duke of Normandy,[6] sent word through two very prominent leaders: Thibaut, count of Blois, and Rotrou, count of Perche, and with many entreaties urged the servant of the Lord to come to Normandy in order to appear physically in person before him. The king apologized that, because of the pressure of various unforeseen events, he did not dare go beyond the limits of his own borders.[7] Bernard agreed, and as soon as the king saw him, the king raised both his hands to Heaven and rendered tremendous thanks to the One who dwells there, namely Christ. After they had embraced one another, the king received him with due honor. After the king had listened to sound religious instruction, he gave many gifts, and in addition he gave fifteen silver marks per year in perpetuity to Bernard's monastery.[8] Because the king felt great love for the confessor of Christ thereafter, he loved Bernard's monks as much throughout his lifetime. Every year, in addition to the income that we mentioned, he sent them sixty or fifty silver marks, more or less, and he earnestly admonished

5. Geoffrey has precisely described the location of the priories that became the future Tironian abbeys of Selkirk/Kelso in Scotland, Saint Dogmael in Wales, and Joug-Dieu in Burgundy/Midi.

6. Henry I, king of England (r. 1100–1135).

7. Henry I crossed to Normandy for Christmas in 1112 and made peace with Fulk, count of Anjou, and with Louis VI, March 23–29, 1113. May 1–3, 1113, Henry I laid siege to the castle of Bellême. In July 1113, Henry I returned to England. See Orderic Vitalis, *Historia ecclesiastica,* 6: Book XI, 45, 180–83; and Hollister, *Henry I,* 230–31. The negotiations might have made him reluctant to go beyond his own borders, but he would have heard about the efficacy of Bernard's prayers from Count Rotrou, who was fighting with him. Henry I returned to Normandy in September 1114.

8. Henry I confirmed Adam de Port's gift of the land of Kington and Beverton in Hereford, on the Welsh border near Offa's Dike, to the monks of Tiron, in 1121–1122 (Merlet, *Cartulaire de Tiron,* 1:29, no. 15 [dated 1117–1126]). The annual gift of fifteen silver marks in perpetuity is supported by a charter issued 1118–November 1120 at Caen (ibid., 1:43, no. 27). His daughter Empress Mathilda increased this gift to twenty marks, and it was confirmed by successive generations of English kings (ibid., 1:109, no. 88; 2:37–38, no. 268; 82–83, no. 309; and 108, no. 331).

them so that there would be no decline in the observance of their religious customs. He also undertook to build our dormitory, royal munificence that entailed many cash outlays.

97. Moreover, after Louis [VI], king of the Franks,[9] the successor of the above-mentioned king, talked with Bernard, he wanted him to have the Saintry property, which we own today, and gave it as a gift.[10] He showed greatest reverence to Bernard's successors[11] after his death, for he wanted his sons, Philip and Louis by name, who later became kings, to receive the sacred rite at the font from them,[12] and he gave countless good things

9. Louis VI (1081–1137), the son of Philip I and his repudiated wife, Bertha, succeeded his father in 1098. He greatly strengthened the power of the French monarch over Ile-de-France and Orléanais. He waged war against Henry I of England in 1104–1113 and 1116–1120. He married his son by Adelaide of Maurienne, Louis VII, to Eleanor of Aquitaine, heiress of Duke William X, in 1137.

10. After his marriage to Queen Adelaide in 1115, Louis VI gave Tiron Abbey four carucates of land at Saintry (Cintry), southwest of Orléans, outside Epieds-en-Beauce near Beaugency, together with some forest rights in the wood of Melleroy. Count Rotrou appears as a witness. Merlet, *Cartulaire de Tiron,* 1:16, no. 5; 18, no. 7; and 2:268 and 285. The priory of Saint George of Saintry was founded there.

11. One of Bernard's successors was Hugh, a monk of the monastery, who is mentioned in Verdon, ed., *Chronique de Saint-Maixent,* 184–87, under the year 1116, and is named as abbot of Tiron in Merlet, *Cartulaire de Tiron,* 1:28–29, no. 14. Probably Hugh was an interim abbot while Bernard's second successor, Ralph, was being recalled from Selkirk. Ralph is named as abbot of Tiron in the Chronicle of Melrose and in the mortuary roll of Vital of Savigny. See Alan Orr Anderson, *Early Sources of Scottish History A.D. 500 to 1286* (Stamford, England: Paul Watkins, 1990), 2:163, citing the Chronicle of Melrose, 66, ca. 1119; and Leopold Delisle, *Rouleaux des Morts du IXe au XVe siècle* (Paris: Jules Renouard, 1866), 323. When Vital's mortuary roll was circulated among many monasteries in modern England and France and passed through Chartres after his death in 1122, the monks of Tiron named only two deceased abbots. They wrote: "Pray for our abbots, Bernard and Ralph, and for all our brothers."

12. Two sons of Louis VI were crowned during their father's lifetime. Philip, born on August 29, 1116, when Hugh was interim abbot of Tiron, was crowned king in 1129 during his father's lifetime and was killed by falling from a horse in 1131. Louis VII was born ca. 1120, at the beginning of the long abbacy of William. Achille Luchaire (*Louis VI le Gros, Annales de sa vie et de son règne* [Geneva: Mégariotis Reprints, 1979], 106, no. 214) records Philip's birth citing the *Annales Sancti Dyonisii,* in *Bibliothèque de l'Ecole des Chartes,* a. 1879, 276, and Louis' birth (ibid., 139, no. 300). Louis VII was crowned king upon his brother's death in 1131, succeeded his father in 1137, and ruled until 1180. Children were customarily baptized soon after their birthdates, which closely fit the tenures of Bernard's successors.

to our monastery until the day of his death. Thibaut, whom we mentioned above, built two priories for us in his lifetime and after his death[13] gave such a profusion of ornaments and other gifts to our church that their large number makes it tedious to list them.[14] Thibaut had the infirmary built at his own expense.[15]

98. It would be equally tedious to list all the others who flocked to see Bernard from various realms and regions, who gave the monks many gifts and properties so that they could build priories, and bestowed good things known only to God. We would like to mention with gratitude William, duke of Aquitaine,[16] Fulk, count of Anjou and subsequently king of Jerusalem, Robert, earl of Gloucester,[17] Henry [William], count of Nevers,[18] Guy the younger, count of Rochefort,[19] William [Henry], earl

13. The antecedent of "his" is unclear and probably refers to Bernard. The varying quality of the Latin allows for the possibility of such weak grammar. Geoffrey repeats the phrase *post ipsius excessum,* which he used in §40 to refer to Abbot Renaud/Reginald's death and in §85 to refer to Bernard's death. Thibaut died in 1152, several years after the death of Geoffrey II, bishop of Chartres, to whom the *vita* is dedicated.

14. Adela, countess of Blois, acted for her son Count Thibaut when she gave land for the future priory of Saint André d'Ecoman (Merlet, *Cartulaire de Tiron,* 1:28–9, no. 14), and Thibaut made substantial gifts to this priory (ibid., 2:116–17, no. 341). She also gave land acting for her son for the priory of Saint-Eutrope de Monrion (ibid., 1:40–41, no. 24). Merlet dates these charters as ca. 1117 and ca. 1119 respectively.

15. Thibaut's natural son Hugh recuperated from wounds at Tiron c. 1136 and professed as a monk there. See Ruth Harwood Cline, "Abbot Hugh: An Overlooked Brother of Henry I, Count of Champagne," *The Catholic Historical Review* 93, no. 3 (July 2007), 506.

16. Merlet, *Cartulaire de Tiron,* 2:274, cites a false charter linking Saint-Léonard-de-Ferrières with a son of the count of Poitiers, but Tiron's cartulary contains no donations of land for priories by William IX and X, dukes of Aquitaine. They may have given cash gifts or valuables.

17. Robert, earl of Gloucester, a natural son of Henry I, witnessed a confirmation of a donation in Nately and Mapledurwell (Hants) granted to them by Adam de Port 1131–1133 (*Winchester College Muniments,* 2:95, nos. 2788 and 2789).

18. The first names of the earl of Warwick and the count of Nevers are inverted. William, count of Nevers, gave a gold vase to Tiron during the famine; see §70.

19. In 1114, Guy, count of Rochefort, gave multure and income at Rochefort, a town in Poitou-Charentes, Charente-Maritime, on the Atlantic coast of Aquitaine south of the port of La Rochelle (Merlet, *Cartulaire de Tiron,* 1:17, no. 6). In 1115 Guy participated with other donors in the gift of a church of Saint-Epagne and various lands at Ablis (ibid., 1:19, no. 8).

of Warwick,[20] Robert FitzMartin,[21] Guichard of Beaujeu,[22] Geoffrey, viscount of Châteaudun,[23] Girard Berlay [of Montreuil-Bellay],[24] Brice of Chillo [Chillou],[25] and many other individuals, whose works we could not cover in a brief account.[26] After

20. Henry of Neubourg, brother of Robert of Beaumont, count of Meulan, earl of Leicester (d. 1118), is not listed as a donor in the cartulary of Tiron, but he was married to Margaret, the sister of Count Rotrou, and probably contributed in some manner to Tiron Abbey. See John T. Appleby, *The Troubled Reign of King Stephen* (London: G. Bell and Sons, 1969), 44; and David Crouch, *The Beaumont Twins: the Roots and Branches of Power in the Twelfth Century,* Cambridge Studies in Medieval Life and Thought, 4th series, 1 (Cambridge: Cambridge University Press, 1986).

21. Robert FitzMartin was the son of Martin des Tours, a Norman knight who came over with William the Conqueror in 1066 and conquered Cemaes, Wales, in 1087. Robert FitzMartin established the "Priory of Wales" (Saint-Dogmael) in the diocese of Saint David's, protected by Cardigan Castle, in 1114–1115. In 1114 Henry invaded Wales, to stabilize the situation created by Welsh challenges to the strong Norman lordships and to install the queen's Norman chaplain Bernard as bishop of Saint-David (1115–1148). Robert's mother donated Caldey Island offshore Tenby in the Channel. See William Farrer, *An Outline Itinerary of King Henry I* (Oxford: Oxford University Press, 1920), 69, no. 323; Emily E. Pritchard, *The History of St. Dogmael's Abbey* (London: Blades, East & Blades, 1907), 24–27, 40–41, and 60–61; and John Edward Lloyd, *A History of Wales from the Earliest Times to the Edwardian Conquest* (London: Longmans: 1967), 2:480–81.

22. Guichard of Beaujeu founded Joug-Dieu in the archdiocese of Lyons and the seigneurie of Beaujolais. The date on the forged charter is June 28, 1118, but presumably the priory was established ca. 1115 during the lifetime of Bernard, since it possessed locks of Bernard's beard (Merlet, *Cartulaire de Tiron,* 1:30–31, no. 16).

23. Geoffrey IV, viscount of Châteaudun, gave the abbey tithes he was owed there on the tonlieu, toll, fodder, his own coins, and salt, ca. 1119 (Merlet, *Cartulaire de Tiron,* 1:37–38, no. 21). In 1131 Viscount Geoffrey gave them a tract at Val-Saint-Aignan and the tract of La Crotte (ibid., 1:175–76, nos. 152 and 153; 2:279 and 310).

24. In 1118 Girard Berlay (of Montreuil-Bellay) gave lands and firewood at the site of the priory and future abbey of Asnières (Merlet, *Cartulaire de Tiron,* 1:35–36, no. 19). Montreuil-Bellay, in Maine-et-Loire, is north of Poitiers and 17.5 kilometers (10.5 miles) north of Thouars.

25. In 1135 Brice of Chillou, whose family seat was at Jaulnay, 17.3 kilometers (10.4 miles) northwest of Châtellerault, founded the priory and future abbey of Bois-Aubry, also known as Saint-Michel de Luzé (Merlet, *Cartulaire de Tiron,* 1:240–41, no. 213). See Christian Gilbert, "L'Abbaye Saint-Michel de Bois-Aubry," *Bulletin Archéologique du Comité des Travaux Historiques et Scientifiques,* new series, 19 (1983): 9, n. 5.

26. Orderic Vitalis (*Historia ecclesiastica,* 4: Book VIII, 27, 330–31) confirms the benefactions of donors of high and low rank from Chartres, Dreux, and Corbonnais.

the death of the man of God, some of those who had already built priories enriched those priories through more taxes and income as well as real estate out of reverence for him, to such an extent that, at their request, we appointed abbots for them. Nonetheless we elevated them on the condition that they and their successors would obey our orders in all things and not refuse to comply with our customs in any way. Just as priors had formerly ruled those priories, these abbots would be subject to laws and regulations instituted by our authority in everything.

99. At that same time Robert, a man of very noble lineage, crossed expanses of the ocean to visit the holy man. Taking thirteen of Bernard's disciples with him, he traveled across the Anglo-Norman borders. When he had come to the outer limits of the region of Wales, to a site on the shore of the Irish Sea near the Teify River, he established a priory first, and later established a monastery suitable for all uses, with an abbot for the same number of chosen monks, on the terms we described.[27] At that same time, after David, [chief] of the men of Lothian and Northampton and later king of Scots,[28] had learned from Rumor of the liv-

27. Robert FitzMartin, mentioned above, founded the priory in Wales that became the abbey of Saint Dogmael in Cemaes, Pembrokeshire.

28. David, the future king of Scotland (1124–1153), was born around 1080–1085, the youngest son of Malcolm III and Saint Margaret. In Alan Orr Anderson, *Scottish Annals from English Chroniclers A.D. 500 to 1286* (London: David Nutt, 1908), 232ff., citing Alfred of Rievaulx, *Epistola,* in Twisden, 347–50, there is a contemporary account of King David's piety. When his sister Mathilda married Henry I of England in 1100, David stayed at Henry's court, where he was employed as a justice. By 1113 he obtained possession of lands from Glasgow to Berwick bequeathed to him by his brother Edgar in 1107. See also Anderson, *Early Sources,* 2:147–8, n. 2. The *Anglo-Saxon Chronicle* version H, 1, states that Henry I "gave the earldom of Northamptonshire to David, the queen's brother, between Christmas [1113] and February 17 [1114]," in Charles Plummer, ed., *Two of the Saxon Chronicles parallel, with supplementary extracts from the others* (Oxford: Clarendon Press, 1892, reprinted 1929, 1952), 1:244–45, At that time Henry I married David to Countess Matilda de Senliz, daughter of Waltheof, earl of Northumbria, who brought David lands, wealth, and the earldom and honor of Huntingdon. See Archibald A. M. Duncan, *Scotland: the Making of a Kingdom,* Edinburgh History of Scotland (Edinburgh: Oliver & Boyd; New York: Barnes and Noble, 1975), 1:134, and Barrow, "From Queen Margaret to David I. Benedictines and Tironians," 30–38.

ing signs of the merits of our most blessed Father, he sent word through most insistent messengers for Bernard to send him a sizeable community of his disciples. In Lothian, which borders on Albania of the Scots on one side and is adjacent to the borders of Northumberland on the other side, he built a monastery for them at a site on the banks of the River Tweed and endowed it with extensive possessions and sufficient income.[29] After David had done so, since he longed to see the man of God, he traveled from the north over the borders of many interlying regions, crossed the vast expanse of the English Channel and the provinces of Normandy, and came to Tiron. Because the holy Father had already died, David could not see the one he wished to meet. David did not wish to seem ungrateful to the monks for whom such a man had been responsible or to have his journey seem purposeless. Laying aside the trappings of his royal dignity, he knelt with due reverence before the grave of Bernard. He gave the monastery he had already founded more taxes and properties, took with him twelve chosen monks with an abbot of the order according to the above-mentioned law, in addition to the monks he already had, endured the very long and tiring journey, and at last reached the provinces of his kingdom.

100. In our writing we have noted the names of these kings, dukes, counts, and noblemen who made sure they saw Bernard, man of God, and increased the possessions of his monastery, but, because they are so numerous, we have touched briefly on only a few of the many donors. If we tried to include all those who multiplied our monastic priories and buildings in various kingdoms, this little book would exceed its limits, and I do not say the fastidious but the more studious reader would find it tedious.

29. Archibald C. Lawrie, *Early Scottish Charters prior to A.D. 1153* (Glasgow: James MacLehose and Sons, 1905), 26–28, no. 35, and 275–76, notes that Selkirk is some miles from the Tweed, but the early endowments of the monks included land by that river at Melrose. More likely Geoffrey conflated Selkirk Abbey with its refoundation in the town of Kelso in 1128 as Kelso Abbey, which overlooks the Tweed opposite Roxburgh.

Who could relate, by name, the hundred priories built for our monastery before this little book was written?[30] Who could describe, using their unpronounceable names,[31] all the places and properties where our priories are located? Who would read such wordy tomes, if such tomes were written, when a series of narratives would be required to describe them?

101. The aforementioned servant of God had such tremendous feelings of sympathy that, if someone confessed a serious crime to him (and a great many people came to him for such reasons), he was as affected as if he had committed the crime himself, so that by his own weeping he moved the criminal to tears. The grace of the Holy Spirit had so imbued Bernard with its sweetness and with steadfastness in prayer and contemplation that Bernard diligently spent the greater part of the day and night in this way. He overflowed with such an abundance of tears while so occupied that anyone who sought to look at his face would virtually see two rivulets streaming from his eyes. The delightful drink of divine sweetness watered him with droplets of the river of God's delights (Ps 36:8), and it made the land of his heart fruitful through the upper springs (Jgs 1:15) and thus encouraged his desire for the bliss of God's elect. When a brother was briefly absent, in his great sorrow he tortured himself by his own laments. If he committed the slightest faults, he lamented them as if they were sins of the deepest dye.[32] Because his mind had grown weary of life, he was inconsolable and wept bitterly that his own life was prolonged. Since he saw the wicked deliriously happy doing evil and exultant when they saw the worst

30. Merlet, *Cartulaire de Tiron,* 2:60–67, nos. 291 and 292. These papal bulls, issued in 1147, confirm the hundred priories.

31. Geoffrey may have been perplexed by the pronunciation of the names of the foundations in the British Isles, such as Mapledurwell, Hants, the site of Andwell priory, or the Scottish priory of Lesmahagow, pronounced "Less-mah-HAY-go," founded by David I in 1144.

32. Jerome, "Ad Eustochium," 15, CSEL 55:326, no. 108, beginning "If he committed."

misdeeds, he wept bitterly about their ruin with brotherly love.

102. Because a superabundance of grace had united his mind with the divine mind with so much feeling and constancy, as the Apostle says: "But he who is united to the Lord becomes one spirit with him" (1 Cor 6:17), his countenance reflected this union in this manner and thus was similar in aspect to that of an angel. Those who observed him thought that he had the face of an angel and that his very countenance shone with sweet clarity. In particular when he celebrated the holy offices of Masses, he used to shed such an abundance of tears, because he was moved by the presence of the body of his Creator, that his own priestly vestments were thoroughly drenched by the torrent. When he blessed the monks, performed the rite for deceased brothers, or sent any of his disciples to distant regions, since his heart was filled with brotherly love, he could not keep from weeping and moved others to tears by his tears.

103. No wonder that he was filled with tears in such great profusion, since the grace of the Holy Spirit granted him increases in all virtues. Prudence[33] flourished within him, such prudence that, whatever he thought or did, he arranged all things according to the rule of reason and willed and did nothing except what was right. He could foresee human acts as if with divine judgments. In contemplation of divine things he disdained the world and all things that are in the world. He directed his soul's entire deliberation solely toward the divine, not as if he were transported by elation but as if he perceived them in his mind by what he alone knew, as if nothing else existed. By fleeing human things he was concerned solely with divine things. His reason, intellect, circumspection, foresight, gentleness, and caution arose from this virtue of prudence. He was so strengthened by fortitude that his soul overcame all fear of misfortune, and he feared nothing except disgraceful conduct. He bore ad-

33. The cardinal virtues are justice, prudence, temperance, and fortitude.

versity or prosperity with fortitude. He was not terrified in the least by the dissolution of the mind and body. Through his virtue of fortitude he wanted not to conquer his vices but to know none, so that then he would not experience the vices of irascible persons and would not desire anything. Fortitude gave him magnificence, nobility of character, faithfulness, composure, tolerance, firmness, and constancy.

104. Temperance kept him within bounds, so that he had no desire to punish and did not exceed the law of moderation in anything. He subjugated all bodily needs under the yoke of reason, insofar as nature allowed, and therefore he disregarded them all and did not repress earthly desires but seemed to consign them totally to oblivion. Thus modesty, shyness, abstinence, chastity, honesty, moderation, shamefacedness, frugality, and sobriety were engendered within him. Justice prevailed so strongly over him, however, that he rendered to every man (Rom 2:6) what was his own. His observance of each virtue made him concentrate on the singleness of his purpose. His mind's purpose was attuned to the divine mind, and through emulation he forged a perpetual covenant with it. Undoubtedly the virtue of justice was the source of his innocence, friendship, concord, compassion, piety, love, and humility.

CHAPTER 12

At the Point of Death: Two Exhortations to His Monks, Reception of the Deathbed Sacrament

105. Bernard was like fragrant *nard,*[1] not by chance but I reckon by Highest Providence, as was shown by the very letters of his name. The fragrance of his many virtues continuously scented the idleness of earthly depravity with a whiff of most delicate odors, like smoke from aromatic myrrh and frankincense ascending from the desert of this life or like a concentrated abundance of powdered spices of every kind. Yet the end was fast approaching, the end that the Creator and Redeemer of the human race, generous rewarder of His athletes, wished to bring to Bernard's multiple and tremendous labors, and on the eleventh day after His Resurrection[2] the burden of the flesh was invited to its inestimable reward. What more can I say? Confident of Divine Clemency, in which his spirit trusted, of course, knowing its utter purity, after he left the Sunday[3] service (which he attended with his disciples at night time) he went out of the church alone and

1. Geoffrey is playing on Ber*nard* and *nard,* believed to be spikenard, *Nardostachys jatamansi,* an ancient aromatic plant. Jesus is anointed with nard in Mark 14:3 and John 12:3.

2. Easter Day fell on April 2, 1116. Eleven days later, Wednesday, April 12, 1116, Bernard had a premonition of his death.

3. Sunday, April 16, 1116.

through the cloister door, without summoning help. O sorrow! He was thrown to the ground disease-stricken and succumbed to a very serious sickness. He began to realize that he was on the point of leaving us. Several of our number became concerned that he had left the chanting choir and had not returned, which was not his custom. They followed him, looked here and there, and found him lying in that place. He never failed to observe the canonical hours both day and night on account of any earthly reason or any powerful personage, although he was interrupted very frequently while he lived, nor was he detained by any burden of the flesh, except this once, when the happy man finished the happy race (2 Tm 4:7). He was first or among the first who always did his utmost to attend these services until they were concluded, and he encouraged others to imitate him more by example than by fear, in a proper fatherly spirit. With deep heartfelt sighs, they carried Bernard to a small house in the opposite direction, turning over in their minds what had just occurred.

106. After the psalms had been chanted according to custom, the crowd of monks, soon to be bereft of the presence of such a great patron, ran around in circles looking for him, weeping and heedless of their steps. When they could not find the one they sought they wept inconsolably. O! How his absence, which as I said was momentary, caused unbelievable desolation in the assembled community at the prospect of his death and left them deeply grief-stricken! What did you perceive, sorrowing flock? Why do you weep for one whom you have not yet lost? What sorrow has stricken you? What made you aware of the secrets of God? The shepherd is not yet stricken, and you are looking for a place to scatter (Zec 13:7, Mt 26:31, Mk 14:27). If you are lamenting now because he has been gone for an hour, I suppose that when you are certain he is gone you all will be desolate. The shepherd of your community is mortal, and no one can escape the laws of mortality. After the most holy Father had had no physical strength for some time, mainly by his own order he

was carried into the chapter by the hands of others. With what strength he possessed he spoke to his sons, who were lamenting inconsolably, and tried to moderate their grief by elaborate rational arguments. He demonstrated repeatedly to them that they were opposing Providence by their sorrow at his passing, but he could not restrain the force of their love and sorrow by the laws of reason.

107. The most holy Father began to speak these words in order to curb their sorrowful laments: "Fear not, little flock, for it is your Father's good pleasure to give you the kingdom (Lk 12:32). If you are mindful of my most humble poverty, and if you are willing to follow the examples and regulations I set for you, and if you reject other ways, when I am dead the constant oppressive lack of material things will not weigh so heavily on you, God willing. Therefore, dearly beloved, let the laws that you have learned be enough for you. Do not seek other ones or search for better ones. Do not presume to reject those orthodox customs of the one to whose instructions you freely submitted, for Christ's sake. For you did not choose me, but I chose you (Jn 15:16), and I did not enter into your labor (Jn 4:38), but you unhesitatingly entered into mine. Accept all that you do not yet perceive except by what is heard (Rom 10:17), believe me, as a man of experience, give ear (Ws 6:2) to me, as you should, my beloved. I am not giving you a stone instead of bread, or a scorpion instead of an egg, or, as God is my witness, a serpent instead of a fish (Lk 11:11–12; Mt 7: 9–10). Although I have no doubt that you will backslide a great many times, nonetheless I am fully discharging my obligation. I am not saying this to trouble you, but I am trying to forewarn you, my dearly beloved sons. Do not wholly reject the faltering admonition of your veteran Father; unless by chance you find it repugnant to be imitators of the poor Christ (1 Cor 11:1) himself, the priest who was crucified for you. If you scorn to obey the one who proclaimed: Learn from me; for I am gentle and lowly of heart (Mt 11:29), since servants are not greater

than their master (Jn 15:20), you will fall into grave error. When I am gone, I can relieve your needs better than I can while present here in the exile of this utterly wretched pilgrimage. You will know the forcefulness of my argument in the heavenly court, so that after my death you will not suffer so much from such a lack of temporal things. The more the servant is allowed to become familiar with his master's secrets, the more effectively he can help his fellow servants in his own house."

108. He shared the lovely treasure on his lips with them all. He described the joy of Heaven, its quantity, its quality, and for whom it is prepared. He did not pass over Hell in silence and the torments for those therein. He demonstrated by clear reasoning that eternal bliss, rightly promised to beginners, is given only to those who persevere. He counseled that no one should lose hope in the Lord's mercies (*RB* 4:74). He foretold the shrewd deceptions of the Old and terribly cunning Enemy, and he described many new and old ploys so that we could compile them briefly, not as many as he could have described with his intellect and eloquence, but as many as he knew his lamenting flock could bear. He said: "Brothers, since I have been mindful unto death of the salvation of your souls, perhaps I seemed annoying and difficult to you. For that reason, if anyone has a grievance about anything, I implore you to forgive me, and, if perhaps our severity was excessive in any way, to pray that the Lord may not impute it to me as iniquity" (Ps 32:2). When the blessed man said that with tearful sobs, all together they fell on their knees, and they cried out of one accord that he had always been honorable, always discreet, always affable, and appropriately vigilant about everyone's salvation. After saying a tearful farewell, he was carried back by the brothers, and he who hitherto by apostolic authority customarily rejoiced with those who rejoice wept with those who weep (Rom 12:15) from brotherly love.

109. Yes indeed, against all hope, governed and helped by his anticipation of God's mercy, he derived greater strength of soul

from his bodily infirmity. As he became more abstemious the weaker he grew, he thought continually about eternal salvation, while he entrusted his body's salvation to the will of the Lord. His little body, emaciated by his incredible abstinence and severe fasting, was tormented. Some persons believe that in eating penitential foods they are extremely frugal; and even if they surfeit themselves with them, they still fancy their chastity safe.[4] Yet, although when others were sick he freely gave them every indulgence and refused nothing that was needed because of his limited resources; what he counted as austerity in others he counted as indulgence in himself.[5] No young man of sound and vigorous constitution could have delivered himself up to a regimen so rigid as that imposed upon himself by him whose physical powers age had impaired and enfeebled.[6] When many highly respected persons who flocked around him on all sides asked him to restore himself by eating richer food, he replied: "We know that banquets sustain life but cannot bestow health." If a longing to fill one's belly is considered a cure for illness, why do people who feast daily on rich banquets fall ill?

110. To the physicians who were trying to persuade him to take deep baths, he said: "They are not to prepare any baths; shouldn't a mortal man die at the end of his life span? If death is close, they cannot drive it away by immersion in warm water. Why would you entreat me in order to persuade me at the end to relax the rigorous observance in profession that I have long kept?" I admit that in this he was too determined, refusing to spare himself in old age or to listen to advice.[7] The careful reader may say that my words are an invective rather than a eulogy. I call that Jesus whom he served and whom I desire to serve to

4. Jerome, "Ad Eustochium," 17, CSEL 55:329, no. 108, beginning "Some persons believe."

5. Ibid., 20, CSEL 55:336, no. 108, beginning "Yet, although when others."

6. Ibid., 21, CSEL 55:336–37, no. 108, beginning "No young man."

7. Ibid., CSEL 55:337, no. 108, beginning "I admit."

be my witness that so far from unduly eulogizing him or deprecating him I tell the truth about him as one Christian writing of another; and that what were faults in him might well be virtues in others less saintly. I speak thus of his faults to satisfy my own feelings and the passionate regret of us all, who love him still and deplore his loss.[8] We do not grieve that we have lost this perfect man; rather we thank God that we have had him, nay that we have him still.[9] However, he has finished his race, he has kept the faith (2 Tm 4:7), and now he enjoys the crown of righteousness (2 Tm 4:8). He follows the Lamb wherever he goes (Rv 14:4). He is satisfied with good things because he hungered (Mt 5:6, Lk 6:21). With joy does he sing: "as we have heard, so we have seen in the city of the Lord of hosts, in the city of our God" (Ps 48:8). O blessed change! He wept so that now he may always laugh (Lk 6:21); he thirsted so that he might find the fountain of the Lord (Rv 21:6). Whether he felt pain, whether he burned with fever, whether he fell faint, amid all the cruel suffering caused by his bodily infirmities he was covered with the coarsest garments and never changed them for better ones, but now he is clothed in white raiment, and can say: "Thou hast loosed my sackcloth and clothed me with gladness" (Ps 30:11).[10]

111. Thus he bore his illness patiently and practiced abstinence with humility. Since he thought that all he had done was not enough, he longed to do better from day to day. Amid the painful stinging, which he bore with wondrous patience, unmindful of his age and frailness of body, he would not allow himself to be placed on any soft bed, and poor in spirit followed the Lord in His poverty to death, giving back to Him what he had received and becoming poor for His sake.[11] We know that

8. Ibid., CSEL 55:338, no. 108, beginning "The careful reader."

9. Ibid., 1, CSEL 55:306, no. 108, beginning "We do not grieve."

10. Ibid., 22, CSEL 55:338, no. 108, beginning "However, he has finished his race."

11. Ibid., 15, CSEL 55:327, no. 108, beginning "and poor in spirit."

many persons while they have given alms have yet given nothing which touches their bodily comfort; they aided the poor and needy (Ez 16:49) but are themselves overcome with sensual indulgences; outwardly they were whitewashed but within they were full of dead men's bones (Mt 23:27). Bernard was not one of these. His self-restraint was so great at the time of his own death as to be almost immoderate; and his fasts and hard bed were so severe as to almost weaken his constitution.[12] The commiserating and compassionate Lord, who supported the purpose of Bernard's heart with heavenly aid, kept him so steadfast that the burning stinging could not wring one moan from him. As he was pierced with repeated stabbing pain, with tears he offered thanks for the crowning touch of virtue. What am I doing? But I must not neglect to proceed with my narrative or, as many perceive, dwell too long upon a single point forgetful of the rules of writing.[13] Envy always follows in the track of virtue: it is ever the mountain top that is smitten by the lightning. It is not surprising that I declare this of men and women, when the jealousy (Acts 13:45) of the Pharisees succeeded in crucifying the Lord Himself. All the saints have had illwishers, and even Paradise was not free from the serpent (Gn 3) through whose envy death came into the world (Ws 2:24).[14] I am a witness to that very Truth, and His holy angels, even the guardian angel who accompanied the admirable man, would have me say nothing in his favor like a flatterer except what I have said as a witness. I have understated the merits of someone who was praised by the whole world.

112. When he had been ill for five days,[15] the most holy and feeble man was carried into the chapter on the same bed whereon he lay. The blessed follower of the Crucified was set down before the venerated image of the Crucified. Thereupon the

12. Ibid., 17, CSEL 55:328, no. 108, beginning "We know that many."
13. Ibid., 3, CSEL 55:309, no. 108, beginning "What am I doing?"
14. Ibid., 18, CSEL 55:329, no. 108, beginning "Envy always follows."
15. Friday, April 21, 1116.

seasoned veteran addressed the assembled recruits, who were lamenting inconsolably and eagerly listening for a final admonition from their advocate. He told them from the fullness of his heart that love is first among the cardinal virtues, and anyone called up for a great battle for the faith would be wise to give it top priority. Since a disciple is not above his teacher (Mt 10:24, Lk 6:40), words Christ told His followers to bear in mind above all as He was returning to the Father and saying farewell to them on the day before His Passion, the blessed imitator of Christ was not seen to deviate in any way from Him whose place he held (*RB* 2:2), when he too was departing from the world, because he said exactly what was proper with fitting fatherliness to those to whom it was owed. He taught authoritatively how many virtues could be abolished and utterly demolished except for love. He proved by ample evidence that truly it covers a multitude of sins (1 Pt 4:8), it is the truest seal of those who fight for God, and it sums up the divine commandments (Mt 22:37–40). Supported by the divine prophecy of Truth, in keeping with his pronouncements to men, he concluded his address splendidly by saying that love alone distinguishes the disciples of Christ from the secret accomplices of the Antichrist.

113. "In this alone," he said, "men will know that you are disciples of Christ, not if you were outstanding upholders of superstitious traditions, but if you loved one another, for superstitious traditions lead less to edification than to violation. So I deliberately kept you ignorant of them, dearly beloved, because I knew they would be less helpful than harmful to you, for I was subjected to them for a considerable time and imposed them strictly for others to bear over the course of several years. I had no doubt that some of you rightly longed for them, but, since I considered it more salutary to do what the strong yearn for than what the weak run from (*RB* 64:19), I did not give in one bit on many occasions. I avoided useless innovations, by which I would have made you transgressors once again, while I carefully emphasized

the traditions that were essential, like a father for his children. Where there is no law there is no transgression (Rom 4:15)."

114. In this way, by similarly well-ordered documentary proof, he added expertly with what voice he had: "Since I am going the way of all flesh, by the Lord's will, I came to say farewell to you, O my little sons, assisted by the strength of other men, since you can see my own strength is gone. I came because I longed to be in your presence, for now I am to be taken from it, and the time of my departure has come (2 Tm 4:6). Yet, dearly beloved, do not be the least saddened by the absence of our little body. Let me swiftly leave this gymnasium and come to heavenly lands filled with delights. I ask you to turn your sorrow into joy (Jn 16:20). Certainly you should not lament for my dying when you believe I will be reigning with Christ. Truly, because no man is cleansed from filthiness (Ez 24:13), not even an infant that lives for one day on earth (Is 65:20), I ask your pardon, in your great and inestimable mercy, for all the faults I committed in thought, word, and deed, and I humbly entreat you to give me what is owed to all imitators of Christ." This entreaty was followed by sighs, for it seemed outrageous to those who were present and unbelievable to those who were absent.

115. Thereupon he was anointed with holy oil according to custom and fortified by receiving the body and blood of the Lord. Since he had obtained what he requested from those of us who were standing by, after saying farewell with tears and commending his flock to the Greatest Shepherd (Heb 13:20) less by words than by tears, the tender shepherd was carried back to the cell from where he was conveyed. He was followed by a weeping and wailing crowd of disciples. Their tearful outbursts rose on high, together with their sighs and sobs. Proclaiming that they were wretches, orphans, they lamented unchecked: "Alas," they said, "you are dying, most holy Father. Your steadfastness kept us strong, your forcefulness kept us steady; how far will we stagger and fall, how much will we weaken and collapse? Why are you

forsaking us beginners? Why are you scattering those who have not yet gathered? How ruined will we be? What will come of the scattering? What will result from the destruction? How will we get advice on how to live? Or hope? Or health? Or consolation? Under whose auspices will we find refuge? Who now will prevent the wolves in savage rage from tearing into the sheep, once the shepherd is taken away (Jn 10:12)? Who will comfort us in our misery? Above all, who will provide for us?"

CHAPTER 13

Final Preparation for Death. Revelations, Death, Burial

116. With some of them crying out and others lying half-dead on the ground in spasms, the man, who always did good works, was constrained to be of two minds about his preferences, for he did not want to leave his desolate flock or to be kept any longer from the presence of the Supreme Good. O how the man was torn between great compassion and hope of Heaven! Amid those who were carrying candles uplifted in their hands, he said: "Oh God, fairest maker of everything (Eccl 11:5) that is fair, all my desire, and from whom my sighing is not hidden (Ps 38:9), you know how ardently my soul longs to see you and how it languishes in weary exile for love of you. Nonetheless, if you order me to keep on fighting in order to protect your followers, I will not refuse, and I will endure the toil and sweat as long as it pleases you." As he committed himself in all things to what God's will commanded, he longed incessantly for the joy and bliss that were so close.

117. Two days[1] before the man of God went to Heaven, a matron named Mary (who was an extremely close friend because of the good works to which she devoted herself) lit a candle with

1. Sunday, April 23, 1116.

her usual reverence before the relics of many saints, which were kept then in the tower of the castle of Nogent-le-Rotrou, and lay prostrate in prayer before them. Her daughter was a virgin, whom the servant of God had asked the mother to entrust to him so she could be consecrated to Christ. As we said previously, while she was praying, the relics, which were kept in a cist,[2] emitted a loud noise and terrified her. Then she had a vision that a multitude of monks dressed in white were processing from our monastery toward that very tower, which was less than three furlongs[3] away, proceeding like a procession and preceding the man of God, who was distinguished by his priestly vestments. While she waited trembling for the strange vision to end, suddenly the tower shone from the inside as if the sun's rays were enclosed within it. As the splendor gradually increased, Bernard, confessor of the Lord, appeared to the terrified matron, and his presence completely dispelled her terror. He said to her: "Tomorrow hurry to me and bring your daughter with you, for on the next day I shall depart from this world. You may be sure, dearest, that unless you make haste, you will not see me any more." Having said that, the man who had appeared with company in splendor disappeared.

118. When she returned home, she remained speechless for two hours, to the utmost amazement of the neighbors. Since they wanted to know whether some misfortune had befallen her, she finally related the entire vision point by point. On the following day, as the holy man had instructed, she hurried to him as quickly as possible, accompanied by her daughter. They found him among his own. "I came in obedience to your instructions, Father; I brought my daughter with me as you ordered." "Good," the elder replied, "for if you had delayed the least bit, dearly be-

2. A cist is a box or chest for sacred utensils.

3. Six hundred meters (1,980 feet, or .38 mile). The vision shortens the distance between Tiron Abbey and the castle of Saint-John in Nogent-le-Rotrou, which is 12.8 kilometers (7.7 miles).

loved, you would certainly have returned home without my greeting. I want you to entrust your daughter to me unhesitatingly, which you have put off doing thus far." The mother said, "Most willingly, I grant whatever pleases you, Father." Then, while all those standing around were astonished, he took the girl in his hands. After he had blessed them both, he sent each to her own home. After a few days had passed the immaculate girl was at rest and undoubtedly joined the choir of virgins. Nonetheless, by the merits of the holy man, she exchanged the light of the world for everlasting light. O, you were buried in glory and have better than life! What was snatched from earth was sent to Heaven. Truly, I consider it more a resurrection than a death, since she was certainly saved and uncontaminated by sin. How many would gladly make over their worldly goods together with their lives for such an exchange, if by chance they could find a merchant!

119. Since his limbs were growing weak and the hour of death was approaching, the holy man ordered the brothers who were serving him to ease their exhaustion by napping, for they had stayed awake a long time keeping watch over him. They lay down on the ground every which way and began to sleep, but they were awakened by his voice and realized that he was talking with someone. A multitude of monks came in such glory that the dying Bernard was soon filled with joy. His followers drew closer, alert, and tried to get him to disclose what he had seen. He said, "O, what tremendous tenderness! His mercy is so great! Lord, I had heard that he who is humbled for your sake for a time on earth is raised up to you in Heaven, but now by your grace you wished to assure me eternally of what delight is given to those who subjected themselves to our little self. Delightful servitude, when such rewards follow! Truly to serve you is to reign."

120. The most holy Father applauded the vision shown to him by Heaven in this way. At last, with tearful promises, he said, "You will know for certain, dearly beloved, that all the pro-

fessed of this monastery, who have been delivered from their mortal condition and have been given ineffable glory, are most certain of their own salvation and are most uneasy about your own. They appeared to me just now, happy and clad in white and, shortly afterward, added me to their company. While they were inviting me to the Lord's Supper and to reign perpetually with Christ, when you approached they returned saying farewell. Their glittering radiance deflects the sun's rays; their fragrances overwhelm the balsam tree; their beauty surpasses lilies and roses." With tears springing anew, he said: "How blessed are the mothers who bore them! How blessed are the knees that received them! How happy are the breasts they sucked (Jb 3:12, Lk 11:27)!" Those who were present had memories of a monk of whose salvation they were doubtful, and they wanted to know if he had been seen with the others. Bernard said no, saying, "Indeed, he is in torment." In like manner they inquired whether there would be any ending to his suffering. Bernard said: "He is wasting away from terribly severe punishments." Again they pressed Bernard to find out whether and when he might obtain forgiveness, but they could get nothing out of Bernard except that the monk would suffer many tortures. Because we mentioned this monk, we think it fitting to relate briefly how he lived and died.

121. Now, this monk was involved in many crimes and, moreover, although he had not gone through the ranks of holy orders over the course of many years (which is astonishing to say), he had usurped the position of performing priestly functions. When he came to the man of God, he accepted the monastic way of life but nonetheless did not divulge to anyone that he had committed these crimes. After six months, when he was coming to the end of his life, he revealed what he had thus far concealed, received the blessing of the tonsure, which he had not yet obtained, together with the viaticum, and died. Upon his death, with the weather unchangeable and calm, suddenly terrible thun-

der roared, terrifying bolts of lightning struck, a vast torrent of rain fell, and horrendous flames flashed at the same time. The weather became tremendously violent, and all the winds roared there, yet this atmospheric disturbance was not seen or heard by others except those of us who were living in our little huts. The following day when we were gathered together in chapter as was customary, the man of God said to us: "What unbearable distress must lie in store for sinners in Hell, since such violent weather broke upon us on account of a single wretch? The storm in its intensity was not silent about how great his misfortune was. Truly, I saw demons in the night drawing the wretch through the window, and I saw a fierce fight break out among them over his soul, but I was completely ignorant about the outcome of the altercation." The wretch brought such a death upon himself because he did not deserve to be seen as blessed among the rest.

122. Next the man of the Lord, who was reassured by the foretaste of the vision and exhilarated by the joy in store for him, began going over it as if something were compelling him to talk and could scarcely speak of anything except what he had seen and heard. Some of those standing nearby, who were sincerely sorry and distressed about his death, burst out with these words: "We don't like what he is saying. Now he shuns our company while he longs for the fellowship of those he saw." At last Bernard ordered his disciples to come to him all together, and he did his best to instruct them at intervals, strictly according to individual rank. He admonished the priests and other ministers of God to serve the altar as if they had made themselves into living hosts. He exhorted the adolescent boys, whom he had accepted and educated with fatherly kindness, to guard their virginity as if it were a treasure that could never be recovered and to gird themselves with discernment so that they might preserve it inviolate. At the end, he urged the illiterates to protect the purple, hyssop, and blue from rain and violent wind just as if they were the skins or sacks (Lv 11:32) of the tabernacle of the Lord and to return

to the divine office, which they were not attending because they were serving outside.[4]

123. After he had tearfully given the kiss of peace, in order of precedence, Bernard said: "May He who is the kindest consoler of all sorrows provide a worthy shepherd for you henceforth." Yet his heart was rent within him, and it wrestled with grief, as though it were being forcibly separated from parts of himself. The greatness of the torment he had to overcome made all admire his victory the more. Among the cruel hardships which attend prisoners of war in the hands of their enemies, and the pain of an awful death, there is none severer than separation from children.[5] He closed his eyes as though he despised all human things and did not open them until he breathed out his soul.[6] What ails you, page? Why do you shudder to approach his death? At this very instant we compilers are gnawing away at these writings, and I have made my letter longer than it should be already, dreading to come to the end and vainly supposing that by saying nothing of it and by occupying myself with his praises I could postpone the evil day. Hitherto the wind has been all in my favor and my keel has smoothly ploughed through the heaving waves. But now my speech is running on the rocks, the countless billows are mountains high, and imminent shipwreck awaits both you and me. We must needs cry out: "Save, Lord! We are perishing (Lk 8:24, Mt 8:25)!" and "Rouse thyself! Why sleepest thou,

4. The illiterates, who could not read Latin, were the lay brothers of the monastery. The reference is to the ornaments of the church. Blue *(hyacinthus)* and purple *(purpura)* yarn are mentioned frequently in Exodus 25:4–39:28. Jacinth (also *hyacinthus*), a sapphire or a dark-colored amethyst, is mentioned in Revelations 21:20. Hyssop is a mint-like herb used in asperging. Hyssop is mentioned in Psalm 51:7 and Exodus 12:22, where hyssop was dipped in blood and touched on the transom of the door and both door cheeks of Hebrew families so that God would pass over them. Jesus was clad in a purple garment in John 19:2 and given a sponge full of vinegar on a branch of hyssop in John 19:29.

5. Jerome, "Ad Eustochium," 6, CSEL 55:311, no. 108, beginning "Yet his heart was rent."

6. Ibid., 28, CSEL 55:347, no. 108, beginning "He closed his eyes."

O Lord (Ps 44:23?" For who could tell the tale of Bernard's dying with dry eyes?[7]

124. Not many days passed, and lo! the good Lord summoned His faithful servant.[8] The One who was calling him to glory hastened Bernard's death, and, worn out by his labors, Bernard was invited to his reward. The time came for the blessed and welcome compensation for countless moans, for which that tenant, who was about to gather in the fruits of his good work from the bountiful householder (Mt 21:33–34), was to ascend from the present snares of this life to the eternal kingdom. His limbs, which were shattered by happy old age and utterly spent from incredible fasting, he left to Tiron Abbey by hereditary right because he who was poor in Christ owned nothing costlier. He rendered back to Heaven the spirit that Heaven had rendered to him, and by this end he finished the race of his earthly sojourn.

O happy race, whose prize is Paradise!
O happy ending, followed by life unending!
Let the life of the blessed to toil's rewards attest.

O what a good fight you fought, what a swift race you finished, what steadfast faith you kept (2 Tm 4:7), faithful confessor of Christ!

Indeed, with shining titles, you left us, but not bereft,
Part of the vernal dwellers in spring eternal,
Perpetual heirs and fellow heirs of the kingdom of Christ
(Rom 8:17),
Whom Zion, most tranquil, calm city, and still,
Now cherishes and nourishes with joyful flourishes.

O how faithful is He to whom you credited your own toil and sweat, for which now you have been repaid with so much interest. He has found you worthy to hear that desirable, remark-

7. Ibid., 27, CSEL 55:345–46, no. 108, beginning "What ails you, page?"
8. Tuesday, April 25, 1116.

able, incomparable "Well done." On that day He said to you in His most pleasant and kindly tone: "Well done, good and faithful servant, enter into the joy of your master (Mt 25:21, 23)."

O he gladly retires to heavenly choirs.

The course of your joyous sail has now reached the shores of the heavenly Jerusalem. Your ship's anchor, guided auspiciously and directly by its pilot in hope of absolution, has gripped the port of eternity, and

No more on the main, eluding Death's chain,
He reaches the strand of his home port and land.

125. Thereupon, the dead shepherd, carefully attired in priestly vestments as his preeminence required, on a bier, covered with a seemly pall, was conveyed on the shoulders of priests into the church that he himself had founded. Therein he remained for three full days and nights before he was placed in his tomb. Some disciples of his who were sojourning on the property in Beaujeu near the Rhône River learned of his death that same day by the following sign. When Bernard was alive they had taken away locks of his beard for relics, which were reverently placed in a pyxis and which they sometimes dampened with water for health in illness; they used to restore the sick to health by the lotion they obtained. The very hour when the servant of God departed from this life, from the aforementioned pyxis a most wonderful fragrance issued, as if it were a composite of various kinds of scent. By that sweet fragrance the brothers realized the truth of what had occurred, and they mourned for us and for the loss of such a luminary with brotherly love. A monk dwelling in Britain saw his triumphal funeral celebrated in Gaul at that same hour.

126. Meanwhile Rumor, flying all around on the swiftest of wings, reported that the consoler of this land had departed from this world. In groups, grief-stricken priests and clerics, abbots and

monks, counts and nobles from all the neighboring regions and a vast multitude of people from all sides of the property poured in, eager to attend his memorial service, which they considered to be more triumphal than funereal. Not a single monk lurked in the desert or lingered in his cell. Not a single matron wove in her bedroom (Jdt 8:5–6, Eccl 10:20). To each and all it would have seemed sacrilege to have withheld the last tokens of respect from a man so saintly.[9] Nothing kept any pious woman from attending, not public affairs, not the frailty of the sex, not womanly modesty, not domestic concerns, not even any administrative office albeit at the highest level could detain any woman. They all hurried there eagerly, and they added their sorrow to the sorrow, imposed their sighs on the sighs, forced their laments on the laments, and increased the tears by their tears. They were not hurrying toward some ridiculous spectacle roaring with laughter.[10]

[See the Sermon in appendix A.]

9. Jerome, "Ad Eustochium," 29, CSEL 55:348, no. 108, beginning "Not a single monk."

10. Henskens (*Vita,* AASS Apr. 2: 0252A, n. e) notes: "Here Souchet inserts a sermon in which Bernard is compared to the patriarchs, apostles, and martyrs. This sermon is missing in both of our handwritten copies, where nonetheless 'Sermon' is written before paragraph 128. The sermon is also missing in the other manuscripts in Souchet's possession, who rectified the omission by referring to the Papirien codex, where it can be read. It seems to have been an exordium, to which logically a series of analecta of Bernard's virtues was added."

CHAPTER 14

Analecta of Various Deeds Added to the *Vita*

127. If anyone wishes to hear how intolerable it was to Bernard if anything better than the ordinary food was served to him in the refectory, let him hear what Bernard often did. When he entered the kitchen one day, he saw a little pot cooking on the fire with the others. When he asked whose it was, he learned that it was meant for himself, whereupon in considerable indignation he seized it, poured, and mixed it in with the others. Afterward, he sternly rebuked the brother, who had acted on his own. Another time, when he entered the refectory at mealtime, he went to the high table in order to ring the little bell. When he saw bread placed there that was whiter than the others' servings, surreptitiously he seized the bread, concealed it, and put it at the place of an old monk whose bread he took for his own. The brother refectorian, who forgot to put water in Bernard's cup, fell repeatedly at his feet as he confessed his fault and in tears asked for forgiveness. Raising him, the very gentle man of God consoled him kindly by saying: "Do not be so distressed about it, son, for it was not your fault as you thought but happened by the will of God, who disposes in all things. Since He knew I was not in need, He was led to persuade you to omit what was superfluous." No one else took such care to avoid the snares of

gluttony and ostentation. So that he would not be struck by the weapon of vainglory he tasted whatever was put before him, and so as not to indulge his palate he quickly pushed away what he had just tasted.

128. He took solicitous care of the sick and weak, and he paid utmost attention to succoring spiritual illnesses. Since, least of all, he showed no partiality (Acts 10:34, Rom 2:11, *RB* 2:20), he was brightened by his constant pleasant conversations with the poor, and he gave himself up completely to their friendship, which he found exceedingly sweet. A solicitous observer, he did not fail to inquire about the customs, life, and souls of all persons. He considered himself to be a physician sent by God to cure spiritual illnesses more than physical illnesses. Therefore, since he made light of physical illnesses, he would pretend that they did not exist; but since he inquired closely about spiritual malaise, he would endeavor to cure it completely. For he rejoiced chiefly in the salvation of souls, not in the heights of preferment, whereas many make light of their own souls and lighter still of the souls of others. What more shall I say? This heavenly light, which in His compassion the kind Source of Light kindled to illuminate the world, wished to hide in the obscurity of the desert, but Almighty God, whose counsel stands forever, alters the counsel of men (Ps 33:10–11). He disposed otherwise and dispersed Bernard's rays far and wide, so that He lit up the world by the splendor of such a great light.

129. Therefore, inspired by the famous reputation of so brilliant a man, countless people of various nations would hurry toward him as if toward a light set by God Himself in the candelabrum of the Holy Church. By the grace of the Divine Word the admirable servant of God, who restored them within, would admonish them to turn away from the vanities and worldly follies of this fleeting existence. He said that he would not consider a man to be of sound mind if he hesitated to exchange the least for the most, the common for the precious, and the transitory

for the eternal. He said that the pleasures of a brief and transitory life vanish like a dream, and the day of death lies in wait for man, like an enemy, which will plunge evildoers and unbelievers into the pit to burn perpetually with the Devil and his angels but will admit the truly holy from the exile of this life into the glorious liberty of the children of God (Rom 8:21). While the man of God gave this and other similar instruction, so many people attached themselves to him after renouncing worldly vanities that they could justly be said to have changed for the better. This is a change of the right hand of the Most High (Ps 77:10). What could be more wonderful? Bernard was like the passage written in Isaiah, for he was like a watered garden, like a spring of water, whose waters fail not, and the ancient ruins were rebuilt in him, and he raised up the foundations of many generations. Thus he is called the repairer of the breach, the restorer of streets to dwell in (Is 58:11–12). Therefore a kind of great heavenly army was living in the desert, keeping watch for their king to come with hymns and praise.

130. Let anyone say who can if he ever read or heard of a man whose heart overflowed with such an unheard-of abundance of love, for I myself cannot find enough words to tell how very admirable he was. He did not rebuff any of those who came to him; he did not reject anyone who wished to live with him, not the blind, not the lame, not the bandy-legged, not the hunchbacked, not the maimed (Mt 15:30–31); he gathered all alike to his ample bosom, filled with compassion. He did not hesitate to accept men with wives carrying their nursing infants in their arms; he did not rebuff anyone who was weak or contemptible or anyone who was very poor. When wards and orphans heard of it, while they were seeking food by begging or tending herds owned by others in the countryside, they would encourage one another and say, "Let's get away and go to the refuge that takes in everyone." Whensoever he was sitting in the midst of them (I should not feel ashamed, brothers, to tell or have you hear what the most

compassionate man of God was not ashamed to do, for nothing except sin was shameful), therefore let us say: when he was sitting in the midst of them, and he saw these bandy-legged, lame, half-human persons, who were blind or scrofulous, maimed or twisted, he reflected silently and said to himself: "Perhaps these are the humble by whom the Lord puts down the mighty (Lk 1:52), of whom it is said that to such belongs the kingdom of Heaven (Lk 18:16). God chose what is weak in the world to shame the strong (1 Cor 1:27)."

131. When he was consoling them, he would exhort them to bear the troubles of a brief existence with patience for a little longer, saying: "My children, bear it; do not lose heart (Gal 6:9) for a little while, and take comfort hoping in the Lord (Psalms), and none of those who take refuge in him will be condemned (Ps 34:22). The Lord indeed sets the prisoners free; the Lord opens the eyes of the blind. The Lord lifts up those who are bowed down; the Lord loves the righteous (Ps 146:7–8). The Lord makes poor and makes rich; he brings low, he also exalts. He raises up the poor from the dust; he lifts the needy from the ash heap, to make them sit with princes and inherit a seat of honor (1 Sm 2:7–8). The Lord alone is a stronghold for the oppressed, a stronghold in time of trouble (Ps 9:9). Fear the Lord, dearly beloved, for those who fear him have no want (Ps 34:9); and know that: Better is a little that the righteous has than the abundance of many wicked (Ps 37:16) who are laying up treasures and do not even know for whom they are getting them (Mt 6:19, Prv 21:6). Therefore in your hearts sing psalms (Col 3:16) to the Lord, saying: "O Lord, all our longing is known to thee; our sighing is not hidden from thee (Ps 38:9). Hear our cry, draw me up from the desolate pit, out of the miry bog (Ps 40:2). God will wipe away every tear from your eyes (Rv 7:17), and your sorrow will turn into joy (Jn 16:20). You shall be satisfied with beholding His form (Ps 17:15)."

132. O Christ, your faithful and wise servant nourished your

orphans with this kind of bread, he whom you set over your household to give them their portion of food at the proper time (Lk 12:42). By his spiritual food he often eased their destitution, for as was said above, poverty often oppressed them severely. Very frequently it was reported that there was no bread and that his children had no food, yet crowds of people were arriving who could not properly be sent off unfed because they had come from far away. What then? Reader, consider God's most faithful servant with no bread and with people there to be fed, don't you suppose he might be slightly anxious or unsure of what to do? He was not unsure; he did not hesitate, for his faith accustomed him to taking God's extraordinary generosity for granted. So he would blithely promise what he did not have, because he was confident about the goodness of the Almighty and believed that he would actually have it. Although sometimes, with heartfelt concern about the crowds flocking to him, he asked the Lord what the apostles said when the crowds hurried toward the Lord and they did not have anything to feed them: "Lord, send the crowds away to go into the villages and towns and buy food for themselves, because we are in a lonely place," to which the Lord replied: "You give them something to eat (Mt 14:15–16, Mk 6:35–37)," although, as I say, with similar compassion for this multitude of all kinds of people pouring in on all sides, he prayed to the Lord with a contrite heart (Ps 51:17), saying: "Lord, send them away, so they can go to more prosperous places where they can get what they need, for this is a lonely and barren place," he learned directly by divine inspiration what the Lord was prompting him to do in His words to the apostles: "You give them something to eat."

133. So he would confidently invite everyone to a meal whose provider was the Maker of Heaven and earth. O thrice-happy soul, temple of God the Father, throne of Wisdom, resting place of the Holy Spirit, dwelling of the most Holy Trinity! It is right to believe that Divine Grace, which was in you and would act

through you, would reveal to you in advance what it would do. In what spirit did you invite all comers to a meal when you had no bread, unless you could see with spiritual eyes that God would soon provide? For when He gives to the beasts their food, and to the young ravens which cry (Ps 147:9), do you suppose that He would not give a stipend to His soldier and to His comrades-in-arms? Of course He gave and even gave generously in order to astonish everyone, especially pagans and unbelievers. What happened once in the time of Eliseus happened very often here. There is a passage in the Book of Kings about how Samaria was withstanding a siege, but it was endangered by a terrible famine. Since the king felt compassion about the destitution of his deprived citizens, he went to Eliseus, who was aware of his reason for coming and said to him presently: Hear the word of the Lord. Tomorrow about this time a measure of fine meal shall be sold for a shekel and two measures of barley for a shekel, at the gate of Samaria. Then the captain on whose hand the king leaned said these words incredulously: "If the Lord himself should make windows in heaven, could this thing be?" The man of God replied: "You shall see it with your own eyes, but you shall not eat of it (2 Kgs 7:1–2)." Several people who saw it and were curious improperly went to the man of God and, as if they were counseling him, contradicted him by asking him why he agreed to feed so many people of these kinds when he had nothing. He answered them in a sincere and very steadfast tone that they would have God, not himself, to provide for them. He added, "Do you think that He who feeds the beasts of the field and the birds of the air (1 Sm 17:44, Mt 6:26) could forget about man, made to His image and likeness (Gn 1:26)?" These persons, however, who were men of little faith (Mt 6:30, 8:26, 16:8), had no hope that what the man of God promised could be done, if the Lord himself should make windows in heaven.

134. Dearest brothers, do not be put off by his humility and delight in poverty, which he demonstrated so many times. Be-

lieve me, there are many wonderful miracles that he worked by divine power, which insofar as possible he tried to conceal more carefully than a scoundrel would try to hide his crimes. Nonetheless he could not conceal them all, because Divine Love did not want many of them to be concealed, for the benefit of future generations. Yet, dearest brothers, however others may feel, I admire the humble way of life of this most glorious man among the poor of Christ more than the glittering power to work miracles given divinely to him. Miracle-working has cast down many from the pinnacle of angelic life, whereas humility has raised many humble persons to a higher place. The man of God was aware of the dangers of miracle-working and so he loved and practiced humility. Moreover, he avoided working miracles and declined to do so insofar as he was allowed. But whenever did his love not wrench feelings of compassion for the sick and suffering from him?

135. Since, fittingly, we are discussing spiritual illnesses first, what proud or lofty person went to him and did not immediately return modest and humbled? What adulterer or fornicator? What miser or money-lover? What envious or malicious person who listened to him failed to reform and transform immediately afterward? Thieves stopped thieving; the cruel desisted from cruelty; tyrants refrained from tyranny; criminals stopped committing crimes; the rich counted their riches for little and learned that all they had amassed was no refuge for them; the powerful realized that absolute power was not their security but their downfall; lovers of the world understood that they were slaves to vanity. What more shall I say? He opened the eyes of the blind, which were filled with the dust of worldly mire (Ps 40:2), so that they could see the true light; he opened ears, which the Lord lamented were deaf in humankind (Mt 13:15, Rom 11:8), to heavenly song; he led the steps of the lame in the way of peace (Lk 1:79) and justice. If someone had ingested something foul at the Serpent's suggestion and was poisoned, Bernard cured him

by the antidote of Scripture, so that as a spiritual physician he cured the sick by faith, hope, and love (1 Cor 13:13). Who can tell how many persons who were tormented by demons he liberated by his tremendous virtue? How many did the faithful servant extricate from the jaws of the Old Serpent and restore to God? He restored persons to life who had been dead not for two days but for three days or even four days. That is to say, he found out persons who were dead because of their pernicious delight in the lethal thoughts dwelling enclosed in their hearts, or persons who were fatally elated about doing foul deeds, or persons who were trapped by the pitiable habit of sinning or by filthy fantasizing as if they were buried in the earth, and the divine power of heavenly grace did not fail him as he raised them all from this kind of tomb for the dead.

136. These, therefore, are the divine miracles that the Almighty Creator worked through him, which are justly considered more admirable because they are more salutary. These miracles are the ones that liberate the soul with the body from perpetual death and restore it to eternal life. These, therefore, constitute the power to save the world (Jn 12:47), which the Gospel attests that the Savior transmitted to the apostles and to popes. The Savior taught these things; he ordered them made known to the weary world, when he said to his disciples: "Heal the sick, cleanse lepers, give sight to the blind, raise the dead, cast out demons (Mt 10:8, 11:5)." If we interpret the Lord's meaning correctly, we plainly see that He expected his disciples to practice more on souls than on bodies. As the Gospel says, one day when the disciples returned with joy because demons were subject to them, when he saw them abased by vainglorious elation, as if indignant He said to them: "I saw Satan fall like lightning from heaven (Lk 10:17–18)." To those who exulted about healing the sick and casting out demons He was to say at the end: "I do not know where you come from (Lk 13:25, 27)."

137. This most blessed worshipper of God feared to please

men, not to displease sinners, and thought little of exercising the grace of such miracles, which he considered made him be as one with fakers. As was said previously, he refused to succumb to it many times, unless he was compelled by compassion and impelled by all who were suffering from distress and pain. He was not one of those who advance by outdoing themselves in great and wonderful deeds. Why are we dwelling on this? Now at last let us disclose what he hid and reveal what he tried to conceal. For hidden wisdom and unseen treasure, of what value is either (Ecclus 20:30)? So let us say, when was an aching head or another painful limb not eased immediately by the touch of his holy hands? O, how many people I have heard confirm that they experienced it themselves! When was a person who was disturbed by the wiles of the Devil and, after he took refuge with Bernard and confessed what temptations were tormenting him, did not obtain relief and immediately find repose?

138. When a brother (whose name I shall not mention, since he is still alive) was harassed by evil angels with the onset of religious unbelief, he fled troubled to the man of God, confessed his unbearable mental distress, and demanded Bernard's assistance with his most holy prayers. The most merciful servant of God took compassion on his anxiety and distress and said: "Calm down, son, this temptation has not befallen you as a ruination, as you fear, but as an examination, Lord willing. For the most merciful Creator customarily tests His soldiers by temptations. Therefore stay in the contest like a strong athlete who is certain of God's help, for an athlete is not crowned unless he competes according to the rules (2 Tm 2:5)." When the brother replied in tears that the temptation seemed to exceed his strength, the most blessed man said to him: "If you wish to be free of these troubles, go away confident, because God will send you help from the sanctuary (Ps 20:2)." From that hour (as the brother used to tell me himself) he was unassaulted and at peace and was not the least tempted ever again.

139. One time Bernard with his brothers was traveling through a certain village, and in the center they encountered an elegant woman who was elaborately dressed; the servant of God and solicitous shepherd of the sheep noted that some of the brothers very incautiously looked at her. As they went ahead, he said to them: "That woman we met would have been beautiful, if she were not one-eyed." Unaware of what he intended, they answered, "She is not one-eyed; she looked at us clearly with two eyes." Bernard said: "Believe me, dearest brothers, I tried not to look at her long enough to know whether she had one eye or two." When they heard this and realized that they had been tricked by the shrewdness of the very astute man of God, they were ashamed.

140. If anyone wishes to hear again how expertly he tested human minds and corrected them by testing, he should listen to what follows. When there was clamor about Bernard, who was fleeing worldly things, he went to live on that island, which was surrounded by the sea and nowhere near the land, as he earnestly desired and greatly wished. There, free and unoccupied by speaking and reading, completely tireless in contemplation of Heaven, he filled his mind with divine meditation. He had disciples, however, who provided for him materially by the work of their hands, and after prayer, contemplation, and meditation on reading, he would go out to see those workers. One of them was placid in spirit and the other was really impatient, so they did not work together but apart. The wise man studied their characters and cleverly tested them. When he came to the first, he said, "Bless you." Next, as if he wanted to work, he took the iron tool from the brother's hands and told him to rest in the meantime. Carelessly, he dug up clods of earth and threw them every which way, heedless of where or how he ought to place them. He asked the brother if he were doing well, and, since the brother was very well pleased by whatever the holy man did, the brother replied that he was doing excellently. Next, he went to the other disciple and did the same. When Bernard threw the clods around care-

lessly, the other disciple tried impatiently to teach him how he ought to place them.

141. When the most blessed man saw that he could not do as that brother wished, he went away, turned back to the other one, and taught him a bit of Scripture while he worked. When the other disciple saw, he was jealous and complained that Bernard preferred the other disciple to himself. So he went to the venerable man of God and complained in tears that Bernard scorned him and preferred the other to himself, for Bernard consoled the other disciple, taught him, instructed him with divine words, and showed him more affection and himself much less. The experienced man rebuked him and answered by saying: "Why do you ask me why I'm not going to you, brother, when you are displeased with all that I can do? Your impatience shows that I hinder you more than I help you. Since he approves of all I know how to do, his gentleness shows me that I am not hindering him but helping him. So I am right to leave you alone, because I am hindering you, and to go to him, whom I believe I am helping, since he shows me so by thanking me." Stung by the medicine of the expert physician, the brother quickly fell at Bernard's feet, confessed his fault, asked Bernard's forgiveness, which he obtained without difficulty, and thereafter amended his ways. See how shrewdly the most excellent shepherd knew how to snatch straying or lost sheep from the jaws of the wolves!

142. Now we shall include this episode in the text, for we were not urged to be silent. A serf subject to the man of God and the brothers, whom he served, often stole food in order to eat. When the brothers realized it, they placed the food under lock and bolt, but, since the lock was of no use in keeping off the serf's thieving hands, the brothers informed the most holy Father. The man of God was very angry with them: "What is this, what have you done? You are not fraternal but fratricidal! When you were supposed to love him like yourselves, why did you mercilessly drive him into this pit of homicidal ruin? You, I say, you did this, for

you forced your hungry brother to steal when you locked up the bread lest he take it, although Christ never denied you the bread of life. You wicked criminals will bear the blame for this matter unless you quickly come to your senses."[1] The brothers heard, trembling and terrified, fell prostrate on the floor, and, as they begged his pardon and entreated the most holy man, they asked what they ought to do. First Bernard poured out prayers to the Lord for them, and then he said, "Go, remove all the locks, allow the brother to take his food freely and encourage him to take as much as he wishes; I think that love is the only remedy for your evildoing and his." O wisdom, not human but divine, not terrestrial but celestial, not from man but from God, and not of the earth, but of Heaven.[2]

[See Prayer to Blessed Bernard, Appendix B]

1. Bernard's legalistic solution is in keeping with Romans 4:15, *but where there is no law, there is no transgression,* cited in §113, so where there is no lock there is no theft.

2. Henskens (*Vita,* AASS Apr. 2: 0255A, n. c) notes: "A prayer to Blessed Bernard follows, written in the manner of a poem or a response that would customarily be recited in religious offices. Because of its brevity it has been omitted here, as was the case in Souchet's edition."

APPENDIX A

Sermon

According to Henskens, between 1290 and 1297 a monk at Tiron, Jean Pignore de Vallea, made a copy of Geoffrey's three-volume *vita.* Pignore de Vallea divided the work into 70 paragraphs introduced by a synopsis of verses written in Latin hexameters. About three centuries later, Pignore de Vallea's copy of the *vita* was transcribed into a codex prepared by Jean-Papire Masson (1544–1611). The codex also contained a sermon as an epilogue to the *vita.* This sermon stressed Bernard's abandonment of family in Abbeville [5], the number of people who flocked to him and entered his monastery, the legal disputes he had to endure [6], the violence of the original site of Tiron, infested with wild beasts and criminals [8], his preaching and conversion of the local inhabitants [10], the combination of active and contemplative monks in his abbey [12], and his kindness, humility, and charity as an abbot [18]. The sermon expounded upon the meaning of the names of Jacob's wells and compared Bernard to the saints, prophets, and martyrs. It was published as chapter 63 in the Souchet edition.

Sermon

[1] It would be unwise of me to put my hand to a work that I am unworthy to complete, but love, my commander, is compelling me through the heartfelt wishes of some simple brothers, who keep asking me to write something about the venerable and most holy Dom Bernard, our most glorious Father. They say that my writing would be edifying to themselves and many others.

[2] O, how many times have I resisted? How often have I stayed my hand, which was about to write down what my soul was dictating, persuading, repeating, and urging. Yet shyness and presumption forced me to desist, shyness lest a sapphire be ruined by a bad cutter, presumption lest a night owl seem to be speaking of the sun. It is incorrect to serve wine in a clay cup and not a golden one. I acknowledge that I stand in need of correction. I fear no critics, for what can a critic do, when the writer accuses himself of virtually everything? Since for this reason also I am unworthy to order myself to say anything about our most venerable and admirable Father, nonetheless I will relate to you with such eloquence as I possess, not such as I desire, a matter about which I do not wish to remain silent. Great devotion makes a humble task an important one. The woman who put her offering in the treasury was praised by the Lord for her devotion (Mk 12:42–44, Lk 21:2–4). They are asking me to write it for their satisfaction and my own, not for the delights of poetry, but for the edification of their lives. Accordingly I must embark upon this vast ocean because of their wishes and love, and you must pray, dearly beloved, that I can reach port with that same author and governor, for He is my ruler and my helper, my hope and my salvation. Amen.

[3] I would have felt far less trepidation and terror if I were to offend any of the holy fathers of the Old and New Testaments. For I had to consider carefully a man who was like them when I portrayed him in my description, because he embodied the virtues of all the fathers of the Old and New Testaments. I admit that I abandoned the work when I had scarcely begun it, but when I turned my mind upward to the Almighty from whom comes every good endowment, every perfect gift (Jas 1:17), I grew stronger once again. I paid attention, and when He revealed secret things to me, I knew why the man we are discussing, the venerable and most holy Bernard, our most glorious Father, may rightfully be considered an equal to the patriarchs, prophets, apostles, and martyrs. We believe that he was not inferior to them in mercy, compassion, gentleness, or humility; he was firm in faith, upright in hope, steadfast in love, and most persistent with regard to renunciation, poverty, and abasement. Whoever was so polite to the poor (Ecclus 4:8) or was so commiserating toward the weak (1 Cor 9:22)? As I may say briefly, he was wholly devoted to all, rejoic-

ing with those who rejoice (Rom 12:15) and sympathizing with the sorrowful.

[4] Since he may seem to share those virtues with many others, as it were, let us consider his special qualities. Abel is praised because he sacrificed a lamb from his flock of sheep (Gn 4:4) and suffered from his brother's wickedness. Not on one single occasion but always as long as he lived, Bernard sacrificed to God with a pleasing odor (Gn 8:21), not a lamb but, what is greater, his own body mortified to sin. When he was alive, did he not wearily endure the wickedness of many false brethren (Gal 2:4) with compassionate forbearance? At God's command, Noah built the ark, in which he enclosed lambs with wolves, oxen with lions, and other animals that are generally hostile toward one another. The world was submerged, and he allowed them to leave the ark after the flood (Gn 6–8), but nonetheless he could not alter the rapacity in the wolves or the ferocity in the lions. So let us see whether the venerable man whom we are discussing may rightly be considered inferior to Noah.

[5] Noah built the ark of God of gopher wood (Gn 6:14); Bernard sheltered the Church of God through the billowy sea of this life. Noah released the souls of wild beasts whose ferocity was unchanged; by changing the brutish ways of men, Bernard taught them to love one another and would not agree to go away from them. Therefore he may be praised rightfully, proclaimed rightfully, and venerated rightfully. Abraham, complying with the divine command, left his country and kindred and came to the land that the Lord showed to him (Gn 12:1); however our Abraham, that is, the father of a multitude of nations (Gn 17: 4–5), who was predestined by God, abandoned at God's call not only his native land and his parents and people, but also, rejecting all earthly and carnal pleasures, at last came to the place appointed for him by God, led by God Himself. Now what was Abraham promised! I will make of you a great nation (Gn 12:2), and, because you see this promise fulfilled in our most glorious Father himself, it seems inappropriate to try to expand upon it.

[6] Isaac went out to meditate (Gn 24:63) and was walking along the way to the well of One who Sees (Beer-lahai-roi) (Gn 16:14).[1]

1. The author of the sermon used the Latin names of Isaac's wells in the Vulgate and elaborated on their significance in the text.

When he saw Rebecca coming toward him, immediately he united himself in marriage. We should take due note that this passage applies to the most blessed man. While he was diligently meditating in the flowery fields of Holy Scripture, and I do not say he was walking to, but rather he was concentrating on, the well named *One who Sees,* that is, the inner mystery of divine contemplation, he accepted a multitude of people who came running toward him, wishing to suffer any hardship for Christ. That multitude rightly may be named Rebecca, which means patience, with whom he did not unite himself carnally in marriage, but instead, like a fiancé, he took care to link the multitude with himself by a betrothal. It is said that Isaac dug wells, not only the ones that his father had dug, but also new ones, on account of which there were quarrels and contention with the Philistines (Gn 26:14–15, 18). It will not be difficult to see how much of that passage could be applied to our Isaac, since we are aware of the kinds and number of quarrels and disputes that people who were denying the truth made him endure. Since quite a lengthy effort would be necessary to relate them, we will omit them, because we are hastening on to other things.

[7] Therefore Isaac abandoned his wells, stopped and filled with earth (Gn 26:15, 18), to the quarrelsome Philistines and, when he came to Beer-sheba, dug a well; when he found water, he named it Room (Rehoboth), because he said: for now the Lord has made room for us (Gn 26:22) and the Lord appeared and said: I am the God of Abraham your father; fear not, for I am with you (Gn 26:24). His servants dug another well, and, when they found water, they reported it to him. He called it Abundance (Shibah) and the name of that town Beer-sheba (Gn 26:32–33).

[8] After hearing this, dearly beloved, if we understand it, we will rejoice and exult with praises to God, with joy like the joy that Isaac was sent and given by God on such an occasion. We see what we said above, because those who are hateful to God and who deny the truth are quarreling with him. So you must meditate on it. For what reason? Because he wanted to understand what is on high and not what is on earth, he wanted to extricate himself from earthly things and to progress toward heavenly things, and that was to remove the earth that stopped up the wells of their hearts. Since they would not allow it,

he went away from them. He could not stay with those people, who wanted to have earth in wells and not the water of wisdom. Led by the Lord, at last he came to that desert place of Beer-sheba, for God knew beforehand that Beer-sheba would be the future well of sufficiency and Abundance, according to what is said: where sin increased, grace abounded all the more (Rom 5:20). At that time the place was a den of wild beasts, a hiding place for brigands. It was a place of pillaging, murder, and slaughter; no pilgrim, no cleric, no monk could walk there in safety. The athlete of God knew it and, armed with the breastplate of faith and the sword of hope, which is the word of God, and protected by the helmet of salvation (Eph 6:16–17, 1 Thes 5:8), he stood firm, undaunted, leaning on his staff, which was affixed in the ground, as he explored the place in his mind, not with his eyes, because the thick forest and its undergrowth prevented him from gazing far. He was quite impressed with the pleasant solitude of the place and the suitability of the quiet desert. At last he addressed his humble community in this way. "Dearest brothers, the place that we sought with devotion a short time ago is suitable for us and quite adequate; it is suitable for silence, fittingly quiet, and appropriate for divine meditations and prayer. Here the army of Christ may bear its burden, here is the promise of an unfading crown."

[9] They nodded their heads in agreement, prostrated their whole bodies on the ground, and gave thanks to Almighty God, the creator and governor of all. What more can I say? They unloaded Poitevin,[2] for that was the name of the donkey that used to carry packs with the man of God seated on his back. Household goods that were not superfluous were set down, and a cell was constructed that was not very sumptuous or skillfully crafted. Without delay, Rumor flew to warn the Gentiles that Saracens had appeared and taken possession of Authou,[3] as if it were an ancient city. Indeed, Authou is now leveled to the ground, and its ancient ruins may be seen today in that place. What the local neighbors heard from Rumor frightened them, on ac-

2. Bernard's donkey is mentioned but not named in the *vita,* §55 and §66. The donkey's name, Poitevin, refers to the city of Poitiers, where Bernard's abbey of Saint-Cyprien was located.

3. Saint-Denis d'Authou is a town located 3.9 kilometers (2.3 miles) north of Thiron-Gardais, so Authou may be an earlier settlement at that site.

count of that donkey. In their fearful imaginings the neighbors said that the men had burst forth from underground caverns and were a fraction of the troop of armed men who were following to ravage them. After this embellishment and others, the neighbors sent scouts who approached and observed unwarlike unarmed men, who were not constructing evil contraptions but were building modest cells, who were not raising castles or towers and were not shrieking war cries but were reciting psalms and hymns.

[10] The scouts returned bearing better reports, beating their criminal breasts, and announced that the monks were not Saracens but new prophets sent by God to abide in the desert. When this news was disclosed, the people, rich and poor alike, hurried there eager to see them. Now the time had come for our Isaac to dig a well. He went out in their midst, addressed the people, and taught them whom they should fear and whom they should serve. He exhorted them to prefer heavenly things to earthly things, to exchange the transitory for the eternal, and this instruction was the well: that is, the removal of earth from the heart of mankind. What ultimately happened? He found wellsprings of spurting water which God put in man when He created him. Man sought to bury the wellsprings in earthly pleasures but not to dry them up completely within himself. Is there anyone completely unendowed with a good nature and totally incapable of doing good for all? Since their minds were prodded repeatedly by the word and example of the man of God, they renounced the world and repented. Therefore Bernard evoked the well named *Room* by saying: "for now the Lord has made room for us, and we shall abound in the land (Gn 26:22)." Therefore, not undeservedly, this place is named Beer-sheba, as we said earlier. Where sin increased, grace abounded all the more (Rom 5:20), in the way of God, by God working through His servant.

[11] Let us incorporate what remains and continue to use analogy in all things. His servants mean his disciples, who dug not so much one well in one location as many wells in many regions, and when they found water they reported it to him. When they returned he called them Abundance, saying: Now the Lord makes us abound on earth (Gn 26:22).

[12] Let us examine, if you please, by what craft and cunning Ja-

cob pilfered Laban's sheep, to see if by chance we can interpret how this great overthrower of sin (Prv 13:6) prevailed against Laban the Devil with no less craft and cunning. Now Laban means whitewashed, which rightly means the Devil, who transfigures himself into the Angel of Light. Therefore let us relate how Jacob took fresh rods of poplar and almond whose bark was partly peeled and partly intact, and he put the rods in the troughs where the sheep were accustomed to drink at the time when they bred, so that at the sight of the rods the flocks brought forth sometimes black and sometimes striped, speckled, and spotted (Gn 30:37–39), as he willed. Our own shepherd knew how to do the same with his sheep. In the troughs, that is, in the sacred writings, where the sheep drink, that is, where the innocent of spirit are refreshed, he put rods, that is, precepts for a rule for an honest and upright life, partly peeled, that is, with the literal cover removed and specially interpreted, and partly with the bark intact, with their literal and historical meaning. He gave men of the flesh milk to drink, according to the Apostle, and urged the spiritual men toward higher things (1 Cor 3:1–2), so that his sheep produced some black lambs, active young, and others white, contemplative young. Some, however, were speckled and spotted, both active and contemplative young.[4] We are touching on this matter briefly, so as not to tire the reader with a wordy exposition. Consider the following.

[13] When Moses led the people of God out of Egypt and into the Promised Land, he removed them a three-days journey from Pharaoh and from Egypt (Ex 15:22), so that in the desert they could sacrifice worthy victims to God, which they could not do in Egypt.

[14] Certainly our lawgiver taught us to extricate ourselves from the power of the Devil, who is called the prince of this world, and from the shadows of laying up worldly goods, symbolized by Egypt, in three days likewise, that is, by knowledge of the Holy Trinity, either by the way of faith, hope, and love (1 Cor 13:13), or by amendment of thought, word, and deed, so that we would sacrifice ourselves to God,

4. See Constable, *The Reformation of the Twelfth Century*, 188–91, for the symbolism of black and white monastic habits. The author of the sermon suggests that the Tironian monasteries included active and contemplative monks who sometimes coexisted on the same premises.

not sheep or goats. Moses led the Israelites from Sin, meaning temptation, to Rephidim (Ex 17:1), which should be interpreted as soundness of judgment. Our leader was distinguished for acting in a better and a more salutary manner, because he led the followers of Christ out of the temptation of this life of tribulation to soundness of judgment. For the one who is found to have been tested by temptation on Judgment Day will have perfect health (Acts 3:16).

[15] Many things are said of Moses, and it would not be difficult (albeit lengthy) to show similar things of our servant of God, but we shall omit them, because we are not tasting everything about everything in advance, but a little bit about individual things.

[16] Consider David, who cannot be omitted, to whom the Lord said, I have found a man after my own heart (1 Sm 13:14) and took him from the sheepfolds; to be the shepherd of Jacob his people, of Israel his inheritance. With upright heart he tended them etc. (Ps 78:70–72). Heed what the Lord says to us, and with a strong hand (Ex 6:1). We believe that he heard the following directly from the Lord: Good and faithful servant (Mt 25:21, 23), See, I have set you this day over nations and over kingdoms, to pluck up and to break down, to destroy and to overthrow, to build and to plant (Jer 1:10). What was he ordered to pluck up and to destroy if not the thorns and caltrops[5] of vices? And what was he ordered to build and to plant? Believe me, the seeds of virtues.

[17] Consider, dearly beloved, whether what he ordered is visible in you, for in you it should be apparent. You are the rich fields, but I fear that what he uprooted from some of your hearts may grow back, and what he built and planted is being plucked up. Believe me, my Lord and dearest brothers, it is unfitting for us to do so. We must not abandon the footsteps of our great patron in the presence of the Almighty and follow the way of others. Therefore do what he ordered and hold fast to what he taught.

[18] With such a light before you, there is no way you can go astray. It has been demonstrated, although not in all points for reasons of length, that he should not be considered inferior to the Patriarchs of

5. A caltrop is an iron ball with four spikes thrown on a roadway and used to obstruct the passage of horses by injuring their hooves.

the Old and other Testaments in any way whatever. He is believed to be similar to the Elders of the New Testament, for he followed the life of an Apostle and Evangelist, and he totally scorned and rejected the vain delights of the world. He bore his cross in emulation of Christ, mortifying his flesh, and while doing justice, he did not fail to show kindness (Mi 6:8). No one in charge of an entire community showed himself to be so indifferent to worldly things in our time. He did not assert his authority as an abbot by elegant vestments, as many do, but by holy ways of life. If in ignorance you would look for elegance, you would not have considered him to be abbot, because, as it is said, not elegant dress but holy life distinguished him from the others. Many people who did not recognize him because they were deceived by the cheapness of his habit would stop him to ask him: "Where is Lord Abbot Bernard?" To them, in soft words, head bowed, because his countenance was humble and his speech was placid, he would reply by saying: "Tell me what you want of him, and I will listen to you on his behalf. If it is absolutely necessary to see him, however, I will show him to you." Whoever was as guarded in speech? He did not wholly come forward, he did not totally conceal himself. There were many, nonetheless, who could easily recognize him by his angelic expression and shining face. In wintertime, at the numbing winter solstice, he sat in the cloister with the others, without a tunic and without leather shoes, covering his nakedness with a shabby cowl. At that time they were afflicted by great poverty in all ways. He, like a good shepherd, who lays down his life for the sheep (Jn 10:11), stripped himself in order to clothe those whose teeth were chattering from the cold whom he expected were about to die. He was a true abbot, a true father, who neglected himself and cared wholly for his sons.

APPENDIX B

Prayer to Blessed Bernard

Around 1600–1650, five handwritten copies of Pignore de Vallea's initial copy of the *vita* were made. Two of these five copies have survived. One, in Paris at the Bibliothèque Nationale de France (BNF Fonds Latin 13788), was prepared around 1630 for Henry of Bourbon, bishop of Meaux and abbot of Tiron and of Saint-Germain-des-Prés. The Paris copy contains a prayer to Blessed Bernard entitled *Oratorio ad Beatum Bernardum.* The other surviving copy of the *vita,* dated 1656, is in Rome at the Biblioteca Apostolica Vaticana, Reginensis 526. It contains the sermon and the prayer.[1] The prayer reflects a sense that Tiron has lapsed from the ideals of its founder.

Prayer to Blessed Bernard

Holy Father of the Monks, famed amid our pettiness,
Incessantly offended by our perniciousness,
As your flock all but lapsed from your standard of holiness,
The merits you obtain are our very last resort,
Who could support the judgment of a righteous court?
Though we should work for money for self-support,
You see the idleness in which we disport.
Declare that we once had you as shepherd for salvation,
We once received your care and religious education,

1. Beck (*Saint-Bernard,* 473) notes that the text of this prayer is contained in the manuscript of the *vita* at Saint-Germain-des-Prés, BNF Ms. lat 13788 and in Souchet's edition.

Although we were in clear and flagrant violation
Of our good Father's rules, you showed us toleration,
Just as you tried to help one for all, formerly,
When in glory with God, keep us in memory,
Shipwrecked far in the depths of this tempestuous sea.
Save us, lead us to port, where salvation's peace will be.
Unite us, Bernard, monks' hope, with the citizens of Paradise,
For God grants all you ask, and your prayers will suffice.
Therefore pray for your brothers, for your promise was precise.
Cause our virtues to increase, eliminate our vice,
For if, seeking judgment, you take no heed for us,
When before the Judge you were supposed to plead for us,
From this time on who will intercede for us?
So spare us, though unworthy, and ask God to suspend
His judgment; our own wills we were taught to bend,
To work for God alone, not Martha but Mary attend,
But fail because of vices we would not amend.
Thus we should be imprisoned, to death be condemned.
But you, our ferryman, your own you will unbind
From a death we cannot flee, and comfort we shall find.
In your presence we beat our breasts with pious heart and mind,
In God's presence we pour out our prayers of every kind.
Though underneath this habit our active lives we mourn,
Yet from the root as many spiritual benefits are born.
Before us they fight on, behind us others are torn.
Evils pile up, and amid them the heart and mind grow worn.
Oh woe! The witch and hedgehog's cave holds us in captivity,
Behold their whelps' fresh traces, reared in its obscurity,
Deceit, and muttering, slander, rancor, and impurity
Successively pervade us, and iniquity.[2]
The locust, hopper, destroyer, and the cutter (Jl 2:25) have now rent
What prudence, fortitude, temperance, and justice in living sent.

2. This line is partially effaced in Souchet's edition, 150, but appears as *"per nos vicissime transeunt et omnis injustitia"* in BNF Ms. lat 13788, f° 129.

Our foes gorge on our spiritual wealth for nourishment,
Our foes seize us like fugitives if they see us repent.
By releasing death's bonds, prepare a way for us to retreat,
Pierce through the foe's jawbone and subdue him beneath your feet,
So we share your full enjoyment of the heavenly seat,
Given that universal grace which alone makes all replete.
Death devours in Hell those wretches who lack grace,
Where they are ground up and perpetually grimace,
And, old in blame, receive new punishments apace;
These burdened souls are never delivered from that place.
Oh blessed land whose King is love and adoration,
Whose dwelling place is everlasting delectation,
Contemplation of the supreme good its whole collation,
Whose citizens feast in eternal celebration.
We hail the land of the living, our hope when exile's ended,
We hail it from afar, and our longing is extended.
Your land is meant for all; no more except you is intended.
Reward us for our labors once we have contended.
Amen.

APPENDIX C

Synopsis of the Life of Holy Bernard, Abbot of Tiron Abbey

A contemporary of Geoffrey may have prepared a separate short work entitled *Brevis Descriptio in Vita beati Bernardi Tironensis abbatis,* or a synopsis of the life of the holy Bernard, abbot of Tiron. A copy of this synopsis has survived as a separate document, contained in a collection of sermons and hagiographical accounts among the Latin manuscripts of the Bibliothèque Nationale de France, Fonds Latin, 584 fols. 78–80. This synopsis draws on material in Geoffrey's *vita* but shortens and distorts it in ways that show how the salient points of the life of Bernard were passing into legend. It begins with a new story about Bernard seeing a devil collecting crumbs and distorts his quarrel with Gervais over a church and with a monk who covered him with invectives [1]. It summarizes his vision of the dead monks in chapter who foretold the deaths of some of his monks [2]. It includes his vision of the Virgin Mary but has her communicate a different message [3]. It briefly covers his association with Robert of Arbrissel and Vital of Savigny and his vision to seek Tiron [4]. It accurately recounts the date of the first Mass at Tiron and repeats his acceptance of more than five hundred monks [5]. It includes the trials of his monks and the shower of roses [6–7]. It devotes a few lines to his sermon on Samson as he exhorted priests not to take wives and distorts the archdeacon's response [8]. It includes Count Rotrou's release from imprisonment by Robert of Bellême and Robert's imprisonment. It attributes to miracle-working relics the prosperity his visit brought the knight Robert. It changes his deathbed vision of monks to an omen of his forthcoming death [9]. It includes the miracle-working locks of his beard in Burgundy [10]. The synopsis shows a crystallization of the legend of Bernard after his death, with an emphasis on the miraculous.

A Synopsis of the Life of the Holy Bernard, Abbot of Tiron, Church of Tiron

[1] We read that Blessed Bernard was born in the region of Ponthieu. As an adolescent, he became a monk and, day by day, endeavored to achieve perfection through discipline. Upon profession he began to strive for humility and patience: through fasts, vigils, and prayers he endeavored to mortify his own flesh. His first office was to be a server in the refectory. When he entered it, he saw a devil under the table collecting crumbs. He challenged the devil and asked him why he presumed to enter and collect crumbs. The devil replied, "To prevent them from being trodden underfoot and lost." The man of God knew immediately that the devil was not concerned about the crumbs being lost but was a terrible threat to the souls of those who were negligently dropping crumbs. Meanwhile Bernard thought of nothing except religion and was made prior of Saint-Savin during the tenure of Abbot Gervais. Not much later, the enemy of humankind sowed discord among them about a certain church which the aforesaid abbot endeavored to purchase with money to add to his possessions. But, so Gervais would not openly commit simony, the blessed man opposed him and contradicted him. For this reason, on the advice of the blessed man, the abbot relinquished the church with a benediction of brotherly peace. One day when a monk rose up against Bernard and covered him with many invectives on account of Gervais, the monk was immediately seized by a demon and expired.

[2] At that time, after Compline, when Bernard was in the oratory as was his custom and afterwards was returning to the dormitory, suddenly he saw a multitude of monks in radiant white sitting in chapter. He entered, bowed, and spoke to them. After asking for their blessing, he sat with them. Then one of these seated blessed men spoke thus: "Dearest brother, we entered religion in this monastery, whose present dissoluteness distresses us, but we rejoice at its renewal

by God working through you, and we give thanks for your holiness. We are informing you that within a brief period of time eighteen of your brothers will be dead." Having said this, they vanished. The father exhorted his sons to repent, and told them about the vision he had seen. But one of the monks mocked him and called him a dreamer. Although the holy man exhorted him to repent, he would not do so. The holy man predicted that this monk would be the first of all to die, and so it happened. Afterward, he predicted to the others their deaths and how they would die, and so it happened.

[3] After that, it happened that one night in the oratory after Compline when he was absorbed in tears and prayers, the Blessed Virgin Mary appeared to him and said, "Be firm, brother, and act manfully, because no one can be saved without effort. God will give you the victors' crowns, so he has determined, and by your efforts many will be saved."

[4] Subsequently he became an associate of Robert of Arbrissel and Vital of Mortain and first founded Savigny. But he was warned by a vision to seek Tiron and to found a monastery there. When he had done so, one day he saw a brightly shining lamp hanging from Heaven and illuminating not only that place but the whole country.

[5] In 1109 on Easter Sunday, during the reign of Ivo, bishop of Chartres, the first Mass was sung in that place. He tried to accept men of various conditions who came seeking profession, so that in a short period of time there were more than five hundred. At the beginning of their profession the bread shortage was so severe that one pound of bread was divided among two, even three or four monks. But the greater the anguish they suffered, the more devotedly they gave thanks to Christ.

[6] One time a monk named Odo was tormented by a demon while the abbot was away. When the father came back shortly and saw the monk, he cured him. One day, when he was in Chartres and it was dinnertime, he saw by the spirit one of his monks, named Gervais, tormented by a devil. He left his meal immediately, called for his horse, rode back to Tiron, and restored the monk to his former health. A priest, who had made profession, used to steal things from the church. One night, when he was in choir, during Matins, he fell down in front of everyone. When he was reprimanded by the father,

he denied the theft. He fell down again and, leaving the monastery, returned to his dregs and joined his concubine.

[7] One day, when a monk had died, a brother saw the valley full of demons, who were coming to steal the brother's soul. But they did not succeed because it was freed by the father's prayers. A monk who had led a holy life died in the monastery. When his body was brought in the church, and the father had been praying for him for a long time, the deceased appeared to him in white garments. The deceased told the father that he was at blessed rest in Paradise. The same day, when the father was blessing some of the brothers, a monk saw wondrously fragrant roses descend upon them, which showed that the blessing of the holy man was pleasing to God.

[8] One time, when he was preaching to priests not to join unchastely with women whom they were taking as wives, he was reproved by an archdeacon, who said it was no concern of monks. The blessed man replied to him, "Have you not read that Samson slew a lion with the jawbone of an ass? Samson may be translated as 'Sun.' That means Christ, who is the sun of justice, who, with the jawbone of the dead ass, that is, of forceful preaching to simple people who are dead because of their vices and desires, but who do not refuse to bear the burden of the commands of God, blocks his own enemies and the adversaries of the church." When he had heard, the archdeacon abandoned his foolishness and restrained the priests from taking wives.

[9] One time it happened that Robert of Bellême captured Count Rotrou, who was the pious founder of the monastery of Tiron. When Rotrou was in prison, he exhorted the blessed man to pray his hardest to the Lord for him. Having prayed, Bernard told him forcefully that he would escape from Robert's prison and that Robert himself would be taken prisoner by Henry, the king of the Angles, and everything turned out as the holy man had predicted. A knight named Robert entertained him one day with great devotion. When the father had left, the knight kept the straw on the bed where he had lain for relics, and subsequently the blades worked many miracles. Before his death, brothers who had led holy lives and had died in the monastery appeared to him shining and predicted that he would be glorified by Christ in the next life and would depart for the kingdom of Heaven. When they had said these words, they vanished. Subsequently he fell

ill and because of the illness was gathered to the Lord on the ides of April. To him be honor in the community of saints. Amen.

[10] Some of his monks dwelling in Burgundy had kept locks of his beard for relics in the local water, and they cured the sick of their illnesses by giving them this water to drink. On the day he died these very locks in Burgundy began to emit a fragrance. Meanwhile, reverend father in Christ, by your holy prayers and in the name of your discipline, diligently uproot the brambles and thistles and, with your kindly hand, cut down the thorn bushes of sinners which choke the fruits of justice, so that, through faith, we may share in that heavenly glory generously given by the one to whom be honor for eternity.

AMEN.

Bibliography

Primary Sources

Ambrose. *Vita S. Agnetis.* In *Acta Sanctorum* (hereafter AASS). Jan. 2. 351–54.

Anderson, Alan Orr. *Scottish Annals from English Chroniclers A.D. 500 to 1286.* London: David Nutt, 1908.

———. *Early Sources of Scottish History A.D. 500 to 1286.* Vol. 2. Stamford, England: Paul Watkins, 1990.

Andreas of Fontevraud. *Vita Altera* of Robert of Arbrissel. AASS. Feb. 3. 0608D–0616E.

Athanasius. *Vita S. Antonii Magni Abbatis.* AASS. Jan. 2. 120–41.

Augustine of Hippo. *De Sanctis Massylitanis Martyribus in Africa.* AASS. Apr. 1. 0821B–0821F.

———. *De Sancto Marcellino, Tribuno et Notario Martyre Carthagine in Africa.* AASS. Apr. 1. 0539C–0542F.

———. *The City of God.* Translated by Henry Bettenson. London: Pelican Books, 1972; Penguin Classics, 1984.

Baudri of Dol. *Vita Prima* of Robert of Arbrissel. AASS. Feb. 3. 0603B–0608C.

Bede. *Bedae Venerabilis Opera. In primam partem Samuehelis libri iv.* Capitula Libri Tertii. Corpus Christianorum, Series Latina. Edited by D. Hurst. Turnhout: Brepols, 1962.

Benedict of Monte Cassino. *The Rule of Saint Benedict.* Ed. Timothy Fry. Collegeville, Minn.: Liturgical Press, 1981.

Bernard of Clairvaux. *S. Bernardi Opera, Epistolae.* Vol. 8. Edited by Jean Leclercq, Charles H. Talbot, and Henri-Marie Rochais. Rome: Editiones Cistercienses, 1977.

Brevis descriptio in vita sancti Bernardi Tironensis abbatis. Bibliothèque Nationale de France (hereafter BNF), Lat. 584, f° 78–80.

Bullarium Cluniacense. Http:www.uni-muenster.de/Fruehmitteralter /Projekte/Cluny/ Bullarium/015.HTM

Damian, Peter. Sermon 68, Natali Virginum Sermo Secundus. In *Sancti Petri Damiani Sermones,* Corpus Christianorum, Continuatio Mediaevalis, 57. Turnhout: Brepols, 1983.

Delisle, Leopold. *Rouleaux des Morts du IXe au XVe siècle.* Paris: Jules Renouard, 1866.

Dugdale, William. *Monasticon Anglicanum.* Vol. 4. London: Longman, 1823.

Dutripon, F. P. *Bibliorum Sacrorum Concordantiae.* Hildesheim: Georg Olms, 1986. Reprint of *Vulgatae Editionis Bibliorum Sacrorum Concordantiae.* 8th ed. Paris: Bloud et Barral, 1880.

Farrer, William. *An Outline Itinerary of King Henry I.* Oxford: Oxford University Press, 1920.

Fronton, John. *Vita, Ivo, Episcopus Cartonensis in Gallia.* AASS. May 5. 0248E–0253D.

Gallia Christiana. Vol. 2. Paris: Palmé, 1873. Vol. 8. Paris: Ex Topographia Regia, 1744.

Geoffrey Grossus. *Vita beati Bernardi Tironiensis autore Gaufredo Grosso.* Manuscripts: Paris: Bibliothèque Nationale de France, Fonds Latin, 13788. ca. 1630. Rome: Bibliotheca Apostolica Vaticana. Reginensis 526. fols. 1–86. Dated 1656.

———. *B. Bernardi fundatoris et primi abbatis SS Trinitatis de Tironio Vita.* Edited by Godefroy Henskens and Daniel Papebroch. AASS. Apr. 2. Antwerp: Joannem Mevrsium, 1643. 0222C–0255A.

———. *B. Bernardi fundatoris et primi abbatis SS Trinitatis de Tironio Vita.* Edited by Jean Baptiste Souchet. Paris: Billaine, 1649. BNF Imprimés. 4° LN27 1680.

———. *Vita Beati Bernardi Fundatoris Congregationis de Tironio in Gallia Auctore Gaufrido Grosso.* Edited by J. P. Migne. *Patrologia Latina* (hereafter PL) 172. Paris: Garnier, 1895. 1362–1446D.

Gregory the Great. *Pastoral Care.* Edited by Johannes Quaesten and Joseph C. Plumpe. Translated by Henry Davis. Ancient Christian Writers, 11. Westminster, Md.: The Newman Press, 1950.

Gregory the Great. *Regula Pastoralis.* CLCLT-6 database. Library of Latin Texts. Turnhout: Brepols, 2006. PL 77: 0026D–0027A.

———. *Vita S. Benedicti.* Dialogues. Book II. AASS. Mar. 3. 0277B–0288B.

Gryson, Roger, ed. *Biblia Sacra juxta Vulgatam Versionem.* Stuttgart: Deutsche Bibelgesellschaft, 1969, 1994.

Hildebert of Lavardin, bishop of Le Mans. *Epistolae.* Book II. PL 171: 0225B–0228B. Nos. 17–18.

Himsworth, Sheila, comp. *Winchester College Muniments.* 3 vols. Chichester: Phillimore, 1984.

Hugh of Amiens, archbishop of Rouen. *Vita Sancti Adjutoris, Monachi Tironensis.* AASS. Apr. 3. 0823F–0825D.

Hugh of Flavigny. *Chronicon Hugonis. Monumenta Germaniae Historica, Scriptores.* Edited by Georgius Heinricus Pertz. Hanover: Brepols, 1848; Stuttgart: Anton Hiersemann, 1992.

Huygens, R. B. C., ed. *Monumenta Vizeliacensia.* Corpus Christianorum, Continuatio Medievale. Turnhout: Brepols, 1976.

Ivo of Chartres. *D. Ivonis Carnotensis Episcopi, Epistolae.* PL 161–62.

———. *Correspondance/Yves de Chartres.* Edited and translated by Jean Leclercq. Les Classiques de l'Histoire de France au Moyen Age. Paris: Belles Lettres, 1949.

Jaffé, Philippus, ed. *Regesta Pontificorum Romanorum.* 2nd ed. 2 vols. Leipzig: 1885–1888.

Jerome. *Alia Vita S. Pauli Primi Eremitae.* AASS. Jan. 1:604–7.

———. *Vita Malchi Monachi Captivi.* AASS. Oct. 9. 0064B–0069F.

———. *Vita S. Hilarionis.* AASS. Oct. 9. 0043E–0059E.

———. "Ad Eustochium Virginem Epitaphium Paulae Matris." *Sancti Eusebii Hieronymi Epistulae, Pars II, Epistulae LXXI–CXX.* Edited by Isodorus Hilberg. Corpus Scriptorum Ecclesiasticorum Latinorum (CSEL). Vol. 55. Vienna, 1996.

Lawrie, Archibald C. *Early Scottish Charters prior to A.D. 1153.* Glasgow: James MacLehose and Sons, 1905.

Lépinois, E., and Lucien Merlet. *Cartulaire de Notre Dame de Chartres.* Vol. 1. Chartres: Garnier, 1862.

Luchaire, Achille. *Louis VI le Gros: Annales de sa vie et de son règne.* Geneva: Mégariotis Reprints, 1979.

Mansi, Johannes Dominicus. *Sacrorum Conciliorum Nova et Amplissima Collectio.* 9th ed. Vol. 20. Paris: H. Welter, 1775, 1902.

Marbod, archdeacon of Angers. *Vita S. Robertus, Abbas Casae-Dei Ordinis Benedictini, in Gallia.* AASS. Apr. 3. 0317C–0326A.

Merlet, Lucien, ed. *Cartulaire de l'Abbaye de la Sainte-Trinité de Tiron.* 2 vols. Chartres: Garnier, 1883.

Metzger, Bruce M., and Roland E. Murphy, eds. *New Oxford Annotated Bible with the Apocryphal/Deuterocanonical Books.* New Revised Standard Version. New York: Oxford University Press, 1991, 1994.

Nalgod. *Vita Majolus, Abbas Cluniacensis in Gallia* (S). AASS. May 2. 0658D–0668E.

Odilo. *Vita III* [*De Sancto Majolo*]. AASS. May 2. 0684E–0690D.

Odo. *Vita Sancti Gregorii Episcopi Turonensis Per Odonem Abbatem, Prologus.* PL 71: 0115.

Orderic Vitalis. *Historia ecclesiastica; The Ecclesiastical History of Orderic Vitalis.* Edited and translated by Marjorie Chibnall. 6 volumes. Oxford Medieval Texts. Oxford: Clarendon Press, 1969–1980.

Ovid. *The Metamorphoses of Ovid.* Translated by Michael Simpson. Amherst: University of Massachusetts Press, 2001.

Plummer, Charles, ed. *Two of the Saxon Chronicles parallel, with supplementary extracts from the others.* Oxford: Clarendon Press, 1892; reprinted 1929, 1952.

Poeck, Dietrich W. *Cluniacensis Ecclesia, Der cluniacensische Klosterverband (10.–12. Jahrhundert.* Münstersche Mittelalter-Schriften, 71. Munich: Wilhelm Fink Verlag, 1998.

Recueil des Historiens des Gaules et de la France. Edited by Michel-Jean-Joseph Brial. New edition. Paris: Palmé, 1877.

Rédet, Louis, ed. *Cartulaire de l'Abbaye de Saint-Cyprien de Poitiers.* Archives Historiques du Poitou, 3. Poitiers: Oudin, 1874.

Robert of Torigni. *Tractatus de immutatione ordinis monachorum.* PL 202: 309–20. *Recueil des Historiens des Gaules et de la France,* 14: 381–82.

Stephen of Fougères. *Vita B. Vitalis Saviniacensis. "Vitae BB. Vitalis et Gaufridi, Primi et Secundi Abbatum Saviniacensium."* Edited by E. P. Sauvage. *Analecta Bollandiana.* 1882. 1:355–90.

Syrus and Aldebaldus. *Alia Vita* [*De Sancto Majolo*]. AASS. May 2. 0684E–0690D.

Urban II. *B. Urbani II Papae, Epistolae et Privilegia.* PL 151:369–70. No. 90.

Venarde, Bruce L. *Robert of Arbrissel, A Medieval Religious Life.* Medieval Texts in Translation. Washington, D.C.: The Catholic University of America Press, 2003.

Verdon, Jean, ed. *La Chronique de Saint-Maixent.* Paris: Belles Lettres, 1979.

White, Carolinne, ed. and trans. *Early Christian Lives.* London: Penguin, 1998.

William of Jumièges. *The Gesta Normannorum Ducum of William of Jumièges, Orderic Vitalis, and Robert of Torigni.* Edited and translated by Elisabeth M. C. van Houts. Oxford Medieval Texts. 2 vols. Oxford: Clarendon Press, 1992–1995.

William of Malmesbury's Chronicle of the Kings of England. Translated by John Sharpe. Edited by J. A. Giles. Bohn's Antiquarian Library. London: Henry G. Bohn, 1847; reprinted New York: AMS Press, 1968.

William of Malmesbury. *Gesta regum Anglorum atque Historia novella recensuit.* Edited by William Stubbs. Rolls Series 90, 2. London: Eyre and Spottiswoode, 1889.

Secondary Sources

L'Abbaye Notre-Dame de Fontgombault (Indre). Lyons: Lescuyer et Fils, 1960.

Angot, Alphonse. *Dictionnaire historique, topographique et biographique de la Mayenne.* 4 vols. Mayenne: Manutention, 1990.

Appleby, John T. *The Troubled Reign of King Stephen.* London: G. Bell and Sons, 1969.

Barrow, G. W. S. "From Queen Margaret to David I. Benedictines and Tironians." *Innes Review* 11 (1960): 22–38.

Barstow, Anne Llewellyn. *Married Priests and the Reforming Papacy: The Eleventh-Century Debates.* Texts and Studies in Religion, 12. New York: Edwin Mellen Press, 1982.

Bascher, Jacques de. "La 'Vita' de Saint Bernard d'Abbeville, Abbé de Saint-Cyprien de Poitiers et de Tiron." *Revue Mabillon* 59 (1975–1980): 411–50.
Beck, Bernard. *Saint-Bernard de Tiron, l'ermite, le moine et le monde.* Cormelles-le-Royal: la Mandragore, 1998.
Beech, George T. "Biography and the Study of 11th Century Society: Bishop Peter II of Poitiers 1087–1115." *Francia* 7 (1979): 101–21.
Berman, Constance Hoffman. *The Cistercian Evolution: The Invention of a Religious Order in Twelfth-Century Europe.* The Middle Ages. Philadelphia: University of Pennsylvania Press, 2000.
Bisson, Thomas N. "Hallucinations of Power: Climates of Fright in the Early Twelfth Century." The Hollister Lecture, delivered at the 23rd International Conference of the Charles Homer Haskins Society, November 5, 2004, Georgetown University, Washington, D.C.
Bouchard, Constance Brittain. *Sword, Miter, and Cloister: Nobility and the Church in Burgundy, 980–1198.* Ithaca, N.Y.: Cornell University Press, 1982.
Cabanes, M., and J. Y. LaGrange. *Tiron et Molineuf.* Dourdan: H. Vial, 1982.
Chibnall, Marjorie. *The World of Orderic Vitalis.* Oxford: Clarendon Press; New York: Oxford University Press, 1984.
Cline, Ruth Harwood. "The Congregation of Tiron in the Twelfth Century: Foundation and Expansion." Ph.D. diss. Georgetown University, 2000.
———. "Abbot Hugh: An Overlooked Brother of Henry I, Count of Champagne." *The Catholic Historical Review* 93, no. 3 (July 2007): 501–16.
———. "*Mutatis Mutandis:* Literary Borrowing in the *Life of Blessed Bernard of Tiron* by Geoffrey Grossus." Paper delivered at the 26th International Conference of the Charles Homer Haskins Society, November 4, 2007, Georgetown University, Washington, D.C.
Constable, Giles. *Monastic Tithes from their Origins to the Twelfth Century.* Cambridge Studies in Medieval Life and Thought, new series, 10. Cambridge: Cambridge University Press, 1964.
———. *The Reformation of the Twelfth Century.* Cambridge: Cambridge University Press, 1996.
Corblet, J. *Hagiographie du diocèse d'Amiens.* Vols. 1 and 4. Paris: J.-B. Dumoulin, and Amiens: Prevost-Allo, 1868 and 1874.
Cowley, F. G. *The Monastic Order in South Wales 1066–1349.* Studies in Welsh History, 1. Cardiff: University of Wales Press, 1977.
Crouch, David. *The Beaumont Twins: The Roots and Branches of Power in the Twelfth Century.* Cambridge Studies in Medieval Life and Thought, 4th series, 1. Cambridge: Cambridge University Press, 1986.
Dictionnaire de Biographie Française. Paris: Librairie Letouzey et Ané, 1933–.
Dictionnaire d'Histoire et de Géographie Ecclesiastiques. Vol. 17. Paris: Letouzey et Ané, 1971.
Douglas, Mary. *Thinking in Circles, An Essay on Ring Composition.* New Haven, Conn.: Yale University Press, 2007

Duncan, Archibald A. M. *Scotland: the Making of a Kingdom.* Edinburgh History of Scotland, 1. Edinburgh: Oliver & Boyd; New York: Barnes and Noble, 1975.

Evergates, Theodore, ed. *Aristocratic Women in Medieval France.* The Middle Ages. Philadelphia: University of Pennsylvania Press, 1999.

Favreau, Robert, et al. *Saint-Savin. L'Abbaye et ses Peintures Murales.* Connaissance et promotion du patromoine de Poitou-Charentes. Poitiers: Val-de-Loire, 1999.

Fliche, Augustin. *Le Règne de Philippe 1er, Roi de France.* Geneva: Slatkine-Megariotis Reprints, 1975.

Gilbert, Christian. "L'Abbaye Saint-Michel de Bois-Aubry." *Bulletin Archéologique du Comité des Travaux Historiques et Scientifiques,* new series, 19 (1983).

Guillemin, Denis. *Thiron, Abbaye Médievale.* Ceton: Amis du Perche, 1999.

Hart, Carol. "Forged in St. Anthony's Fire: Drugs for Migraine." *Modern Drug Discovery* 2, no. 2 (1999): 20–21, 23–24, 28, 31.

Haseldine, Julian. "Epistolography." In *Medieval Latin: An Introduction and Bibliographical Guide,* edited by F. A. C. Mantello and A. G. Rigg, 650–658. Washington, D.C.: The Catholic University of America Press, 1996.

Hollister, C. Warren. *Henry I.* Edited by Amanda Clark Frost. Yale English Monarchs. New Haven, Conn.: Yale University Press, 2001.

Iogna-Prat, Dominique. *Order & Exclusion: Cluny and Christendom Face Heresy, Judaism, and Islam (1000–1150).* Translated by Graham Robert Edwards. Ithaca, N.Y.: Cornell University Press, 2002.

Lackner, Bede K. *The Eleventh Century Background of Cîteaux.* Cistercian Studies, 8. 2nd ed. Washington, D.C.: Cistercian Publication Consortium Press, 1972.

Lawrence, C. H. *Medieval Monasticism: Forms of Religious Life in Western Europe in the Middle Ages.* London: Longman, 1989.

Lekai, Louis Julius. *The Cistercians: Ideals and Reality.* Kent, Ohio: Kent State University Press, 1977.

Lespinasse, René de. *Le Nivernais et les comtes de Nevers.* 3 vols. Paris: 1909–1914.

Leyser, Henrietta. *Hermits and the New Monasticism: A Study of Religious Communities in Western Europe, 1000–1150.* New York: St. Martin's Press, 1984.

Lloyd, John Edward. *A History of Wales from the Earliest Times to the Edwardian Conquest.* 2 vols. London: Longmans, 1967.

LoPrete, Kimberly A. "Adela of Blois: Familial Alliances and Female Lordship." In *Aristocratic Women in Medieval France,* edited by Theodore Evergates, 7–43. Middle Ages. Philadelphia: University of Pennsylvania Press, 1999.

Louandre, François-César. *Histoire d'Abbeville et du Comté de Ponthieu jusqu'en 1789.* 2 vols. Abbeville: Jeunet, 1844.

Mayr-Harting, H. "Functions of a Twelfth-century Recluse." *History* 60 (1975): 337–52.

Niermayer, J. F. *Mediae Latinitatis Lexicon Minus.* Leiden: Brill, 1997.

Poeck, Dietrich W. *Cluniacensis Ecclesia, Der cluniacensische Klosterverband (10.–12. Jahrhundert.* Münstersche Mittelalter-Schriften, 71. Munich: Wilhelm Fink Verlag, 1998.

Pritchard, Emily E. *The History of St. Dogmael's Abbey.* London: Blades, East & Blades, 1907.

Raison, L., and René Niderst. "Le Mouvement Erémitique dans l'Ouest de la France à la Fin du XIe Siècle et au Début du XIIe." *Annales de Bretagne* 55 (1948): 1–46.

Riley-Smith, Jonathan. *The Crusades: A Short History.* New Haven, Conn.: Yale University Press, 1987.

Roesdahl, Else. *The Vikings.* Translated by Susan M. Margeson and Kirsten Williams. London: Penguin Books, 1998.

Rosemann, Philipp W. *Peter Lombard.* Great Medieval Thinkers. Oxford: Oxford University Press, 2004.

Schmitz, Dom Philibert. *Histoire de l'Ordre de Saint Benoît.* Vol. 3. Maredsous: Éditions de Maredsous, 1948.

Simpson, D. P. *Cassell's New Latin Dictionary.* New York: Funk & Wagnalls, 1959.

Thompson, Kathleen. *Power and Border Lordship in Medieval France: The Counts of the Perche 1000–1226.* Royal Historical Society Studies in History, new series Woodbridge, England: The Royal Historical Society; Rochester, N.Y.: Boydell Press, 2002.

van Engen, John. "The 'Crisis of Cenobitism' Reconsidered: Benedictine Monasticism in the Years 1050–1150." *Speculum* 61 (1986): 269–304.

von Walter, Jean. "Bernard de Thiron par J. von Walter." Translated by J. Cahour. *Bulletin de la Commission historique et archéologique de la Mayenne,* 2nd series, 24 (1908): 385–410, and 25 (1909): 17–44.

Walton, John, et al., eds. *The Oxford Companion to Medicine.* Vol. 1. Oxford: Oxford University Press, 1986.

Watkins, Oscar D. *A History of Penance, Being a Study of the Authorities.* 2 vols. New York: Burt Franklin, 1961.

Index

The Life of Blessed Bernard of Tiron was designed and typeset in
Adobe Garamond by Kachergis Book Design of Pittsboro, North Carolina.
It was printed on 60-pound House Natural Smooth and bound
by Sheridan Books of Ann Arbor, Michigan.